New Entrepreneurship
A Guide for the 21st Century

Complied by Andras Nagy

Published by Ancient Wisdom Publication

http://www.andras-nagy.com

Woodland, California, USA

Nagy, Andras.
    New entrepreneurship: a guide for the 21st cen-
tury / compiled by Andras Nagy.
    p. cm.
    Includes index.
    ISBN 978-0-9824994-6-7

1. New business enterprises. 2. Small business -
Management. 3. Stay-at-home mothers -
Employment. 4. Stay-at-home fathers - Employ-
ment. 5. Marketing. 6. Advertising I. Title.

HD2331-2336
658.1141-- N139   2010907076

I like to thank all the participants who contributed articles to this book. Especially, I would like to thank Rob Shelsky who edited and proofread this manuscript.
http://home.earthlink.net/~robngeorge/index.html

Table of Contents

Foreword

In the 1950s, they taught us to work hard, expected job security, and then, maybe one day, a happy retirement would await us because of all our efforts.

The exact opposite happened all over the industrialized world. In the last thirty years, millions of workers have been "downsized" from their jobs. Out of sheer greed and animosity towards the worker, faceless, corporate entities, often with the single stroke of a pen, displaced hundreds of thousands of workers in one go. This happened all for the sake of quarterly profits. The goose that laid the golden egg, the American middle class, was now under attack.

Therefore, this painful lesson taught us that working for others offered no security. It seldom offered good monetary rewards, and usually did not create the contentment and happiness for which we all strove.

Working hard for others is only beneficial for those others. History shows this. Time after time, as soon as the worker wanted his fair share of the success of a company, he got the cold shoulder. The poor worker had become a nuisance. Management took revenge on the rightfully complaining and often vociferous worker, and his unions, by replacing them either with the newly immigrated, or just moving entire industries offshore to foreign locations with cheaper workers.

As the editor of this book, I have direct personal experience in this. I had spent over twenty years in IT, mostly as an independent computer consultant. I constantly faced the threat of outsourcing or having to compete with the new immigrant class who were granted H1B visas and could then take the jobs of the older, tax-paying citizens.

This creates tremendous stress. No amount of money is worth putting up with the uncertainty, personal humiliation, and degradation of this. I made $90 an hour during the height of the dot com boom. I had refused several, full-time, job offers from the newly founded companies, as most of them were frauds and so later disappeared. (For every **eBay** or **Cisco**, there were hundreds of nameless companies with worthless stock options, and which involved working unpaid, 12-hour days.)

After the dot com boom ended, I found myself in Sacramento without work and a new daughter. I could not travel as before in my earlier, single, and "gypsy" days. I knew nothing about running other businesses, or had any idea which business I wished to try. I wanted to get a full-time job, but I was over forty.

I was out of work for three-years. During this time, I experimented with various businesses. The silver lining was I could stay home with my daughter while experimenting with business coaching and writing. Finally, I settled on one business, publishing, that I could do part time, while maintaining a fulltime job that pays benefits and even has a 401K.

Some of the businesses depicted in this book can be run part time. These are my favorites, because you can have a job and insurance coverage, while building something for yourself. Obviously, those who do not have incomes must first worry about putting food on the table, so my long-term strategy of running a business part time may not appeal to them. Therefore, this will often be a determining factor as to which business you end up choosing. I caution you against choosing solely based on money! Do what you love and do not worry about the money. This may seem counterintuitive, but my years of experience show this to be true. Follow your bliss.

When we seek hard enough, often solutions will be found. I advise you to look at your budget, your family situation, and then evaluate your options based on considering the whole range of available possibilities. Do what you love! The money often will follow.

This book has been the product of the contribution of several small business owners, entrepreneurs, and stay-at-home business moms, all of whom have shared with me their experiences of running their businesses from home. The book consists of two parts. The first part describes my favorite businesses you can run from home, and is written by people who actually work for themselves in these businesses. In this way, the book can offer a special insight to the reader.

The purpose of having these brief summaries of several businesses is to help those who know, deep inside, that running a home-based business is what they want to do, but cannot decide which business is right for them.

This section can and will help in finalizing this very important decision for you.

The reasons for starting a home-based business are:
1. Less stress than in the corporate world;
2. Write off part of your home you deem as office space for tax purposes;
3. You cannot be fired. You may lose a customer and hopefully learn from the experience, but you cannot be downsized, outsourced, or fired pre-

retirement, as so many corporate drones; and

4. Freedom and Joy when choosing a field you actually like and enjoy.

The second part of this book is about actually running a small business. Marketing, promotions, organizational structure all covered in the second part. Some businesses are easer to market than others. On purpose, I stayed away from "businesses" such as MLM (Multi-Level Marketing), because they are mainly involved in recruiting and not selling a viable product.

I also stayed away from addressing affiliate marketing. The reason for this is simple; I believe in creating an actual product or a service. If you cannot do that, perhaps you should not be in business. You can try different industries by seeking out part-time jobs, or by being a volunteer. However, it is important that you not start a business just because you need the money. Starting a business, as you will undoubtedly experience, is more involved, it takes time and patience. So ideally, you want to do what you desire in your heart. Again, the money will follow.

Reading this book will be an interactive experience. Along with the printed book, there is our website and blog to solicit reader feedback and new ideas from successful home-based entrepreneurs. I strongly urge you to visit our website and participate actively in areas of your expertise or interest.

This book and blog are a community effort. In sharing ideas, we all benefit. I urge you to leave information on any business-related swindles that you have discovered. This way, others can learn from your experiences and you can learn from theirs.

PART ONE--Business Ideas for the 21st Century

Chapter 1--My Favorite Business Ideas

Wellness Businesses

For the past year, our lawmakers in Washington have debated the state of health care in the United States, what the government's role should be in ascertaining that all Americans have access to adequate healthcare when needed. Though the President signed the bill into law on March 23, 2010, there is still much controversy and uncertainty about what the actual benefits to citizens will be.

Prudent healthcare consumers are wise to take control of their own care and that of their families. Due diligence and research into alternative, holistic forms of treatment, proper forms of exercise in adequate amounts, and better nutrition, can help people live healthier lives.

Holistic Medicine is a term used to describe forms of therapy that aim to treat the patient as a whole person. Instead of treating just an illness, holistic forms of medicine look at the individual's overall mental, physical, and emotional well being.

Practitioners who believe in holistic principles, treat the symptoms of illness, but also look for the underlying causes, and attempt to prevent illness by putting the emphasis on overall health. Each person's body is seen as a series of interdependent parts, and illness is due to an imbalance in the body's systems. Holistic therapies are used to help return the body to its properly balanced state in a noninvasive way, without the use of pharmaceuticals. A term frequently heard is "CAM" (Complementary and Alternative Medicine), which seems to have become the umbrella term for all forms of therapy not falling within the realm of conventional medical treatment.

As more people realize there are alternatives to traditional medicine and the tightly, interwoven, big, pharmaceutical industry, the market for holistic wellness businesses will continue to grow rapidly. By some estimates, the holistic wellness industry is growing by 140% every year, creating great opportunities for small businesses in the field, many of which can be operated from a home base.

Those entrepreneurial people who are interested in holistic principles have a wide range of therapies available to explore. There is, likewise, a wide range of regulatory and licensing requirements, depending upon the specialty (or combination of specialties) that are chosen, as well as the area of residence of the business. Part of the research into the different forms of therapy should be finding out about the licensing or certification requirements in the intended area of holistic medicine. You should check with the local city and/or other government offices for any required business licenses and necessary permits.

Following, are a few well-known areas of Holistic Medicine and many more that are often overlooked:

Acupuncture

Developed over 2,000 years ago in China, acupuncture can help to cure diseases and relieve pain. It involves inserting very thin needles into specific locations, or "meridians" on the body through which the life energy, "qi," flows. This practice therapeutically manipulates circulation. Most acupuncturists receive three to four years of training at a nationally certified school and pass a national exam, but each state has differing requirements. Canada has licensed acupuncturists since 2003, and legality varies by state in Australia. Many other countries do not regulate or license acupuncturists, and there is no required training.

Aromatherapy

Aromatherapy involves the use of "essential" oils that are extracted from plants, flowers, herbs, and fruits to directly stimulate the brain through the sense of smell. These plant oils are used to affect the physical and psychological wellness of the patient. The oils are also used as massage oils to be absorbed into the skin and the bloodstream. In this manner, they can promote healing and a sense of well being for the entire body through a calming, soothing, and stimulating feeling, which helps to rebalance the systems of the body. There currently is no required training or certification required for Aromatherapists, though there are workshops, courses, lectures, and home-study programs to learn aromatherapy from.

Art Therapy

Art Therapy involves using art materials, like paint, chalk, clay, or markers, to create a visual representation of emotions and thoughts. It combines traditional psycho-therapy with psychological aspects of the creative process. Closely related in practice to mental health counseling, and also marriage and family therapists, Art Therapists in the United States become Registered (ATR), Board Certi-fied (ATR-BC), or licensed as an Art Therapist (LCAT), in some states. Many states also require certification as a mental health counselor, as well.

Aquatic Therapy

Aquatic Therapy is physical therapy that is done un-derwater, often in a heated pool. Warm water provides an easier environment for exercise. It reduces body weight by over 90% and decreases impact and stress on the joints. The physical properties of the warm water help patients to heal by relaxing the muscles and allowing them greater mobility without much pain.

Patients get all the benefits of weight-bearing exercise, without the compression and stress that similar exercises on land would cause to the body and the joints. This ther-apy is especially suited to those who suffer from joint injuries, nerve damage, and arthritis. Though licensing is not required for Aquatic Therapists, there are numerous certifications available, depending upon which type of aquatic therapy is to be offered.

Popular certifications are those from the Arthritis Foundation (AFAP) and the Aquatic Therapy & Rehabili-tation Industry Certification (ATRIC). There are also certifications for those wishing to be aquatic fitness in-structors, and the best known is Aquatic Exercise

Association (AEA.) In addition, of course, you will need a swimming pool.

Ayurveda

Pronounced, "ah-yur-VAH-dah," this is the alternative medical system developed in India, and it evolved without the influence of Western medicine. Ayurveda's process is to integrate mind, body, and spirit with a comprehensive holistic regimen that emphasizes diet and exercise, meditation, herbal preparations, breathing, and physical therapy. Some of the Ayurvedic methods are also used independently, such as the use of massage, herbs, and Yoga.

Ayurvedic medicine has been growing in popularity due to the very popular Deepak Chopra, M.D., who combines traditional medicine with Ayurveda, and frequently talks about it on television. Training for Ayurveda practitioners in India consists of undergraduate and postgraduate colleges, with up to five years of study. There is currently no national licensing or certification standards for Ayurvedic medicine in the United States or Canada.

Bowenwork

Bowenwork is a manual therapy that consists of gentle moves performed over tendons, nerve bundles, and muscles. These movements stimulate the nervous system to activate and send signals to the brain, overriding conscious thoughts and movements, and directly stimulating the body's healing mechanisms.

Unlike massage, Bowenwork uses minimal touch. The practitioner makes gentle and precise moves to reset the body's systems, and bring it into balance. There is no particular license required for Bowenwork, but it often falls under the massage therapy licensing. Massage therapists are required to be licensed or certified in almost all states.

Breathwork

The last 30 years has seen a rapid increase in the blending of ancient breathing techniques with therapeutic practices like massage therapy, psychology, and physical therapy. Breathwork has long been known to optimize health and spiritual awareness. But nowadays, it is also used to clear negative thought patterns, discourage bad habits, and release energy blockages. It is also a completely integrated part of other nonwestern techniques, such as Yoga, Tai Chi, and Pranayama. While there is no licensing currently required, it is important to get training from a qualified instructor, and different levels of certification are available.

Chiropractic

Chiropractors focus on the relationship between the body's structure (primarily, the spine), and function. Chiropractors use manipulative therapy to correct misalignments of spinal vertebrae, which they believe interfere with the flow of "nerve energy" from brain to the body's cells. Restoring vertebrae to their correct places allows the brain's energy to flow through and heal the diseased condition. Training for Chiropractors is a four-year program that includes coursework and direct experience in caring for patients. Licensing is through each state's chiropractic board.

Colon Hydrotherapy (Colonic)

Colon Hydrotherapy is the process of flushing out the colon by use of a sustained flow of warm water. The warm water flushes the fecal matter into a closed system. The process is also called colonic irrigation, and is similar to an enema, though much more extensive. The FDA regulates production of the equipment used in Colon Hydrotherapy, but doesn't regulate their use. Costs for the equipment can be anywhere from $1,200 to $5,000. Currently, only the State of Florida requires hydrotherapists to be licensed, but most practitioners undergo a voluntary certification process.

CranioSacral Therapy

CranioSacral Therapy involves manipulating the cranial bones--the spine, the skull, and its cranial diaphragms, sutures, and fascia. Practitioners say this removes restrictions in the nerve passages and allows free movement of cerebrospinal fluid through the spinal cord, optimizing the spinal bones, and their realignment. The therapy is most often used in conjunction with chiropractic, massage therapy, occupational therapy, and osteopathy. Treatment for TMJ syndrome, fibromyalgia, neck and back pain, migraines, and mental stress is often done with CranioSacral

Therapy. Licensing is required in most states for any sort of massage therapy.

Feng Shui

Pronounced, "fung schway," this ancient Chinese art teaches a person to create harmony in their life through awareness of surroundings. Instruction offers efficient and practical guidance to adjust both internal and external environments for balance, and harmony, for overall physical and emotional wellbeing. Feng Shui certification is available from a number of schools around the country. The cost can vary from $300 to $7,000. This amount depends on how long, and how in-depth the program is, and the quality of the instructors. Many people combine Feng Shui principles with organizing and interior decorating. Licensing generally is not required.

Herbalist

Herbalists use natural substances, like herbs, spices, and plant materials to treat diseases and medical conditions. Certificate and diploma programs available are through some universities and community colleges, as well as alternative medicine schools. Students learn to prepare herbal remedies, such as tinctures, infusions, and extracts. Herbalists practicing in the United States typically don't need a license, as long as they avoid claiming to treat or cure diseases, which puts them in the position of practicing medicine without a license.

Holistic Nutritionist

Holistic Nutrition uses alternative methods of keeping patients healthy, including herbs, organic methods, and sometimes supplements, as needed. People with the knowledge to provide advice on eating and living holistically can provide guidance to those who need it, and demand for them is increasing. While there is no standard certification or licensing procedure offered, nutritionists should check with their state credential boards for laws regarding using the title "Nutritionist," or "Nutrition Counselor." There are, however, a number of schools, both brick and mortar, and online, which can give you the knowledge to provide nutritional advice.

Hypnotherapy

Hypnosis is often used to address a variety of physical, mental, and emotional issues by inducing a state of concentration and relaxation. Hypnotherapy can modify a person's behavior, attitudes, and a wide range of conditions such as dysfunctional habits, stress-related illnesses, anxiety, pain management, and personal development. Training requirements vary greatly around the world, and in many regions, there are no regulations, so in theory, anyone can begin practicing. In the United States, a diploma from a state licensed school is the highest level of official state government recognition. However, in four states, Washington, Indiana, Colorado, and Connecticut, registration or licensing is required

Iridology

Iridology is the analysis of structures and patterns within the eye's iris, which is the part of the eye that controls the diameter and size of the pupils and the amount of light reaching the pupil. This analysis will help to identify areas of inflammation and stages of weakness, or inflammation throughout the body. Professional-grade, iridology equipment can be quite expensive, and might be a deterrent to someone wishing to start a practice. Neither the United States nor Canada requires licensing. However, a number of schools and organizations provide certification.

Massage Therapy

Massage Therapy involves kneading or rubbing a part of the body. Massage is used to increase circulation, to make joints and muscles more flexible. A massage can reduce blood pressure, boost the body's immune system, and help relieve pain and stress. Almost every state requires licensing, and there is a national certification program available. Building a practice might take a little time. Many MassageTherapists also incorporate other elements of holistic medicine, such as aromatherapy in their practice, as well. There are also opportunities to work for spas and clinics.

Meditation

Meditation is an elevated state of awareness and the actual word comes from a couple of Latin words: *meditari* (to dwell upon, think, and exercise the brain), and *mederi* (to heal.) The Sanskrit derivative of the word, *medha*, translates, literally, to "wisdom." Training ranges from one-day programs, to one-year ones. Colleges as prestigious as Harvard University offer such training. Other training courses base their training on religious tradition, whereby students can formally train within a Buddhist or other type of religion, and have a specific set of requirements for certification. Still others offer training in meditation and relaxation therapies, with a psycho spiritual focus. Most Meditation Therapists have their own practice, though they may work in tandem with other holistic care practitioners. At the current time, there is no formal education or licensing required for Meditation Therapists who will use and/or teach meditation as a mind-body treatment.

Reiki

Pronounced, "ray key," this is a Japanese therapy for relaxation and stress reduction that promotes healing. The word "Reiki" is composed of two Japanese words--*Rei* meaning "God's wisdom" or the "higher power," and *Ki* meaning "life force energy." So the word actually means "spiritually guided life force energy." Reiki is a simple technique to learn, and the ability to use it is transferred to each student during a Reiki class. The Reiki Master passes on the ability during an "attunement," which allows the student to tap into an unlimited supply of "Ki" when needed to improve health and quality of life.

This treatment consists of the practitioner placing hands on or near the client's body in a series of positions, usually around the head or shoulders, feet, or stomach, or more specific areas if needed. Positions are held for three to twelve minutes, based on how much "Ki" the person may need. There are many Reiki institutions where you can enroll to get training. You want to be certain you are learning from a Reiki Master. Though there is no state or local license required to practice Reiki, it might be included in the individual state's massage therapy licensing laws.

Tai Chi

Tai Chi is a traditional form of Chinese mind/body exercise and meditation. Tai Chi uses slow sets of body movements, as well as controlled breathing, combining mental concentration, slow and even breathing, and dance-like movements to increase chi (life energy). Tai Chi can be used to improve flexibility, balance, muscle strength, and overall health. Tai Chi is often called "moving meditation" due to the series of slow, gentle, and aware moves, along with deep breathing.

In the United States, Tai Chi teachers do not need to be licensed, and there is no federal government or state regulation. Traditionally, a Master Teacher leads Tai Chi instruction. Training programs vary and there is no standard program. However, there are schools in the country where students can learn from Master Teachers, thereby becoming masters, as well. Currently, training programs vary, with some training programs awarding certificates, and some offering weekend workshops. There is no standard training for instructors.

Yoga

Yoga is more than just an exercise; it is a mind-body practice with its origins in ancient Indian philosophy. With many different styles used for health purposes, they have a few commonalities. Each typically combines physical postures, meditation, and breathing techniques. They involve using a conscious mental process and a set of techniques, like focusing on a specific object or maintaining a certain posture for a period of time. This is to relax both the mind and body by suspending the endless stream of thoughts. The practice of Yoga is growing dramatically in the United States. It is becoming more commonplace to use it for a variety of health issues, and to help achieve relaxation and fitness.

There are training programs for Yoga Instructors all around the country. The programs can last from just days to as long as two years, depending upon the style of Yoga and level of certification attained. Many organizations register teachers and training schools that have met minimum standards, such as requiring at least 200 hours or training, with a certain number of those hours in specific subject areas, such as anatomy, teaching methodology, techniques, and philosophy.

Despite this level of registration, there is no official licensing requirements for Yoga Instructors in the United States. (One exception is that the State of Michigan requires licensing of training schools for Yoga teachers.)

As you can see, there is a wide range of holistic medicine and many opportunities for someone to start a business based on any one, or a combination of, the above-listed therapies. Planning can start with researching some of the major areas of interest and finding out the details on certification, training, and any licensing necessary, as well as the opportunities available to practitioners in any given region.

Green Business Ideas

Going Green simply means making better everyday choices and taking actions that have a positive impact on our environment. Starting a business that helps others to do the same thing multiplies your efforts and helps our environment exponentially. For those who are interested in taking their love of our planet to a new level, here are some ideas for green businesses.

Chlorine-Free Pool Maintenance

The process of keeping swimming pools clear and clean is not difficult, but it can be time consuming, and the chemicals used have traditionally been expensive and unhealthy. Many pool owners have made the switch to chlorine-free swimming pools by using saltwater systems, which naturally clean the pool and leave the water feeling softer and more refreshing. In fact, nine out of ten new swimming pools are saltwater pools. Capitalize on this new trend by starting a chlorine-free pool maintenance business.

You can start this business with little startup capital. You will need to learn all you can about the systems and their maintenance, perhaps by getting some hands-on experience working with your own pool, or working with someone else to learn the ropes.

You will also need a good selection of cleaning poles, nets, hoses, skimmers, test kits, and a large enough vehicle to carry all of your equipment. Check with the local health department to find out if you need certification in pool maintenance. (In some states this may be required.)

Water Filtration and Distribution

Water is big business, but all of those individual 20-ounce water bottles are horrible for the environment. However, many people will not drink tap water or the water they get from their wells, feeling that the taste is not up to par with the filtered water. This creates enormous opportunities for people interested in a water business, as with water filtration or distribution (sans plastic bottles) or a combination of both of them.

There are opportunities to install purification systems for people to use at home. These can be locally installed to run to a certain tap or bottleless cooler, or can be set up so that it purifies the water for the entire home. You will need some basic plumbing skills for these types of installation.

For homeowners who are not ready to make the financial commitment to install their own system, bottled water is an alternative. Reverse osmosis systems can be installed in your home or another location to purify the water, and distribution in large, glass, cooler bottles is environmentally friendly and economical.

You can offer regular delivery of these filled bottles, and you might even add water cooler rentals or sales to your business. Your initial investment will consist of a filtration system, and the costs for an adequate number of bottles to get started. A nice gift for new customers would be some of the safe, refillable, water bottles that do not leach chemicals. These should have your business name and information on them.

Biodiesel Conversion Kits

For those with some mechanical, welding, or electrical skills and knowledge, starting a business converting vehicles to run on biodiesel can be a good source of profit as energy resources become more strained.

There are two different types of conversion kits available, both of them requiring the addition of an alternative fuel tank and fuel system. There are dual-tank kits, which are relatively easy to install, but vehicles equipped with these still have some difficulties on cold mornings. Waiting for the oil to warm up and lower the viscosity can be difficult.

More technologically advanced systems are now being produced, and have been installed on thousands of cars in Germany. These newer systems use only one tank and can run on SVO (Straight Vegetable Oil,) biodiesel, petrodiesel fuel, or any combination of the three. The three German companies that produce the kits say those who are technically skilled can install the kits successfully. This means being able to work on engines, have mechanic's tools, be able to follow wiring diagrams, and have, or have access to, an injector pressure tester (0-400 bar.)

A related business could be producing and selling

biodiesel fuels. Dealers are already selling equipment for home use (makes 20 to 40 gallons a day), or for businesses (capable of producing more than 1,000 gallons per day).

Solar Businesses

The desire to move towards alternative and renewable energy sources is improving the technology dramatically and increasing opportunities in the solar energy field. There are a number of business opportunities, which can be started in the field with little initial investment and limited training.

Solar Panel Installers

Solar panel installers will typically have a background in construction and knowledge of alternative energy. Each state has different regulations and some might require a contractor's license with alternative energy endorsement. Others may have different requirements for this type of business.

The market for solar panels is truly wide open at this point. Now that the equipment is much better than in years past, it has become a viable and reliable source of energy. The customer base is no longer just for people concerned about the environment, but also for other people who are simply looking to save money on their electric bills.

Income projections for this type of business are in the high range, though location, competition, and other factors can influence the business revenue. In some areas, there may already be other companies installing solar panels, but keep in mind that the government and energy companies might soon be the biggest competitors in this field. Location of the business is important, as some states have the perfect weather to collect a lot of energy from solar panels. Florida and Arizona have the optimal climate, and areas that are very rainy or snowy, with lots of cloud cover, will obviously be less conducive to this type of business. Also, research which states offer the best incentives for opening new businesses, especially green businesses. Equally important, are the widely differing range of incentives available for installing solar equipment, as these will encourage consumers to convert some, or all, of their energy needs to solar panels.

Solar tubes

Solar tubes are a low-cost alternative to skylights. Basically, solar tubes are mini-skylights that come in a range of sizes and come packaged complete with everything needed: roof flashing, finishing ring for the interior, installation hardware, and expandable tunnel.

This is a great startup business, because the tubes are easy to install, no permits or special tools are needed, and they cost the homeowner less than $600, including installation and the product, while bringing in as much natural light as a traditional skylight. They can add a tremendous amount of light to otherwise dark areas, like stairways, hallways, and closets.

The installation is completed in a day. Since this is a relatively new product, the growth potential is excellent and there currently is very limited competition. Build yourself a mobile showroom in a trailer with no outside light except that which is generated by the solar tube, and use this as your sales tool. People will be amazed at the amount of light it brings in.

You will need basic knowledge of construction and simple power tools to install solar tubes. There are currently no regulations for installation.

Solar Attic Fans

Attic fans reduce heat build-up and save you money on heating and cooling by displacing hot air with cooler air drawn in through lower intake vents. Technology has advanced to the degree that solar attic fans can be installed right out of the box, with no electric wiring, no permits, and no expensive electricians. These fans are powered totally by solar energy, and are quiet, efficient, and environmentally friendly.

To install solar attic fans, you need to have basic construction skills and power tools, as well as a sturdy ladder to get on roofs. You will also need a vehicle to transport your equipment. Solar attic fans are a relatively new technology with a lot of growth potential and right now, limited competition.

Solar Generator and Solar Oven Rental At Campgrounds

Camping is once again growing in popularity. People accustomed to living green at home would most likely want to continue doing so on a camping trip, if only they did not have to lug along all the equipment to do it.

Renting solar equipment, like solar generators and solar ovens at campgrounds, can interest both people who already know about and use the equipment, and those who are curious about how these things work. By renting solar generators and ovens, people can see how easy they are to use, and how much money they could save at home.

You cannot only make a profit, but can recruit folks to the green army!

Get started by talking with the parks about your plan. You will need permission from the campgrounds to solicit their customers, and some parks will welcome your services, because of forest fire concerns. Keep extra equipment on hand for those people who are so impressed, they would love to buy some and take it home with them.

Your competition is rental, gas-powered generators, and of course, those who sell wood for campfires. If you point out the logical advantages of solar power generators, some people will definitely convert, especially after they have gotten a taste of having to refuel standard generators in the middle of the night.

Eco-Friendly Businesses

Well Drilling

As more people look for earth friendly ways to live and strive to be more self-sufficient, opportunities in well drilling for water will grow. The equipment necessary to start a business of this type has evolved over the years to the point where it is now possible for one person to easily transport and operate the equipment. While a substantial capital investment in the equipment is still necessary, it can be a fraction of what the costs were just twenty years ago.

Equipment to drill wells up to 600 feet deep is now available in so compact a form, as to fit into a full-sized pickup truck, or on a trailer. The equipment needed can now also be found in the pre-owned market, with many websites devoted to just such types of equipment. A rotary drill is the most common type of equipment used, and this performs just like its name implies, by drilling through the ground until it hits the groundwater, which is usually just 100 to 200 feet down.

Of course, there are further considerations, and more experience is required for working in some areas, as in rocky soils or mountainous regions. Find out all you can about the groundwater industry in your intended area.

Most states regulate well drilling, pump installation, and repairs. Many require an examination of the principal's knowledge of the business before issuing a certificate of registration or license to the contractor. Obviously, studying the process and getting some hands-on experience before starting your own drilling business, will benefit you immensely in this regard. Be certain you also have adequate insurance in the event something goes wrong.

Green Cleaning

You can start a business cleaning service using all natural products and a commitment to recycling materials. Green cleaning will help your clients by reducing their carbon footprints, producing financial savings, and even reducing the time lost by employees who suffer due to Sick Building Syndrome. When toxic chemicals are used for cleaning in our airtight buildings and homes, the VOC's (Volatile Organic Compounds) are trapped and even re-circulated by our heating and air conditioning systems. This can harm some people's health.

Starting this type of company requires a commitment to all natural products and a true desire to help the environment. As with all startup businesses, check with your local government to find out which permits or licenses are required, and also secure a good business insurance policy. Other costs will be those for the actual green cleaning products, cleaning equipment, and a vehicle, or vehicles to transport workers, equipment, and supplies.

Carbon Offset Sales and Kiosks

San Francisco's airport made news in September 2009 when they allowed carbon offset kiosks to be installed. Travelers can now swipe their credit card and alleviate their guilt over the carbon emissions due to their flight. In theory, carbon offset credits are used for green improvements, such as tree plantings, solar power plants, and wind farms. Carbon offset credits are, in essence, promises to use money in a way that will reduce carbon emissions. The market for carbon-offset credits is various businesses, governments, and other entities that use them to comply with caps on the amount of carbon dioxide they are permitted to emit.

Small businesses or companies involved in reducing carbon emissions, or which produce low emissions themselves, can sell carbon credits on the Chicago Climate Exchange (CCX). Businesses that might be eligible to sell credits include logging companies, solar power businesses, and companies that do not produce carbon emissions, or produce low emissions. Approval by CCX is required, as is proof of eligible activity.

While the thought behind this is earth-friendly, critics point out that it is not being regulated enough to know if the money used to purchase the carbon offsets is being effectively used. For those small companies expecting a massive new source of income, that just is not the reality at this point, as CCX financial instruments are selling between $.10 and $.20 per metric ton, down from the $7.00 high of May 2008. At this point, consumer and market confidence in carbon-offset instruments is almost nonexistent. This may not be a business worth looking into until and unless major changes are made to it.

Organic Farming

As the call to buy locally grown produce becomes louder, farmers' markets are popping up in almost every little town, and you can easily take advantage of this new movement. You do not need acres of land to produce good, hearty vegetables without the use of chemicals. Organic farmers have a good knowledge of crop rotation, making natural compost, soil nutrition, non-chemical pest and weed control, and proper harvesting and storage of crops. An organic farming business can be started with mostly sweat equity and just a small amount of financial capital. Selling at farmers' markets is typically free, and many add home-baked goods to the mix to increase their profit.

A variation on standard organic farming is greenhouse

farming. Greenhouse farming can yield significant profits, and is a business in which you can make a good living. Of course, the money it takes to get the greenhouse built and running will be significant, as well. Consideration should be given to local ordinances, (e.g., where you can build, etc.), what to grow, how the greenhouse functions, and to whom you can then sell the products. Checking out co-ops in the area is a good idea, as they allow small farmers to join with other farmers, and thus sell in bulk to grocers and other, larger stores.

Reusable Shopping Bags

With the growing backlash against all those billions of disposable shopping bags that end up in our landfills, demand for reusable shopping bags has multiplied enormously. This trend slows the depletion of oil caused by making all that plastic, and it helps to keep those plastic bags from spoiling the environment, both on land and at sea.

You can produce reusable bags from a wide range of eco-friendly materials, such as cotton, hemp, or recycled materials. Start small by stitching up your bags at home and selling them locally (farmer's markets, and small mom-and-pop stores come to mind as great places to sell them), or via the Internet. These reusable bags are simple to make, and there is no limit to the demand for new and creative designs. Growth opportunities are excellent. Reusable bags can be fitted with logos, messages and names of business owners to function as specialty advertising items. (For details, see my Specialty

Advertising Business)

Recycling Business

Every family throws away their share of the 250 million tons of waste produced by the United States each year. This is not only a waste of money, but it consumes valuable resources, not to mention the major environmental problems it also causes. It is a big problem, but also a big opportunity for people who find new uses for things we currently throw away, by giving them another life.

Conventional recycling of newspapers, cans, and bottles, now generally handled by municipal or county trash collectors, is excellent, but does not go far enough. Creative entrepreneurs are repurposing other materials and keeping them out of landfills. A couple of ideas:

You could salvage building materials, such as bricks and wood or plumbing fixtures, such as sinks and toilets, to use in remodeling and construction. Build doghouses out of salvaged wood and roofing shingles. Create art from any type of recycled material and sell it. Alternatively, you could recycle furniture, creating something new from something old. A new cover and new stuffing can make an aging sofa look good as new. A coat of fresh paint can go a long way toward reviving wood furniture.

You can recycle by redesigning old clothes, or making pet beds out of them. Use more shredded old clothes as the filling for these.

The biggest resource you need for this type of business

is time, some skills, and a lot of creativity!

Green Internet stores

Running an Internet store from home allows a global market reach with much lower startup costs than a brick and mortar store. You will still need a lot of time and energy to get started, and the amount of money you make will depend on what you sell. (You might start your store with reusable shopping bags you make yourself, or some of your creative, repurposed furniture.)

Startup costs will be for the products, as well as for getting your site up and running, and ready for e-commerce. You will also have costs for marketing your site (unless you have the knowledge to do that yourself), and shipping products.

Another alternative might be eco-stores that offer a turnkey system with lots of products. Such turnkeys take care of inventory, shipping, billing, and collection. This can be a way of getting started in the business sooner, rather than taking the extra time to put things together on your own. These businesses typically will charge an initial fee in the $2,000 to $3,000 range.

Chapter 2--Consulting Businesses

Bookkeeper

This business is just about as recession proof as possible. Bookkeeping services and tax preparations are necessary in good times or bad. As a bookkeeper, you will work primarily with small businesses, as a data entry person. Your tasks will also include creating reports and accurate, safe recordkeeping.

Startup Cost

Starting up as a bookkeeper is relatively inexpensive. General home office equipment and bookkeeping software, such as **Quicken QuickBooks**, are necessary. I would estimate a startup cost at $1,500, including fax machine, dedicated phone line, Internet, office furniture, and software. If you must purchase a new computer, this estimate, of course, could rise a bit. A reliable car is also helpful, as you often will visit clients to collect their monthly ledgers and receipts.

License/Legal Requirements

There is no licensing requirement for this business. As a tax preparer, some states license the people who can prepare and submit tax returns for others. Check your state's requirement on this. **QuickBooks** offers certification and training in use of their software. You might want to check into the benefits of being a licensed, **QuickBooks** expert.

Education/Experience

You will need to understand and be able to practice basic accounting principles, how they apply to keeping records and detailed files on all pertinent transactions. A two-year accounting community college will be very helpful, but not necessary. If you are detail oriented and reliable, you can begin this business even while taking classes.

There is a company in Utah (Universal Accounting) that offers a course in bookkeeping. My wife, who is a CPA now, took this course, and she claims it was a good experience. It was about a $1,000 (a bit pricy, but it teaches aspects of running a bookkeeping business you will not find in the curriculum of a community college).

Your tasks will be routine and somewhat tedious. Being reliable and detail oriented is more important than expertise in accounting.

Detailed Notes

As a bookkeeper, you must decide how you will charge your clients. One way, would be to charge by the hour. However, experienced bookkeepers usually prefer to estimate the amount of transaction a business will have and charge by the month, based on such transactions, as well as, perhaps, on the need to meet face to face with the client, or other such factors.

Electronic recordkeeping overtook the old paper and

file systems, and unless your client insists on using that, you will be wise to steer them towards the 21st Century and save some trees in the process. Use a flash memory card (preferred) or a read/write CD/DVD disk to maintain the client's records. Some clients must have in-house records; others have no problem with you storing their data for them. Make sure you understand the client's needs in this matter and communicate with them on this before you undertake their business.

Marketing

Many businesses keep paper records and have no concept of computers. Moreover, many bookkeepers for small businesses feel alienated by the idea of computerization and electronic records. Your task, unless you also prefer the paper trail, will be to convince the new client of the benefits of efficient and safe electronic record keeping. This, of course, assumes you are well versed and knowledgeable on the topic.

It is also a good idea as a bookkeeper to be a tax preparer. Check with your state's H&R Block office for education and seasonal hiring opportunities. They are one of the few companies that still hire seasonal help before the peak of the tax season.

Sending out flyers, or membership in the local Chamber of Commerce are two of the standard methods for "putting the word out" of your new service. Personalized door hangers (see, Advertising Specialty Businesses) are good and low-pressure ways to market/promote your new venture.

There are also forums for stock traders/investors. Some

will accept sponsorship. That is, for a price, they will allow you to advertise on their forums. Since transactions for traders are tedious to maintain and some broker firms do not offer efficient ways to transport records to **Quick-Books**, you just might be able to get some business from advertising at such forums.

Computer Consultant

On the surface, this business is similar to being a computer programmer or any other freelance professional of that technological field. However, a closer look will explain the distinct differences of a computer consulting business from other computer and technology related businesses.

A computer consultant has a list of business clients who either cannot afford to, or just do not want to maintain in-house professionals or experts in the myriad fields of office technology. Instead, these businesses would rather pay an hourly, or more typically, a monthly fee for management and consulting services. These services may include data storage, backup, or any other maintenance, such as website updates or data server maintenance. Usually, these consultants avoid coding and programming chores and instead prefer regularly occurring maintenance tasks, whether hardware or software related.

Startup Cost

The startup cost includes the need for a working car that is well maintained, a laptop computer, and a cell phone. Most people already have these or have ready access to them, so although the cost will vary from person to person, it usually should not be too high. Laptops and cell phones, nowadays, are virtually interchangeable with the advent of 3GL Networks and with the smart phones that Apple and Google came out recently. Personally, I would prefer a cheap cell phone with a nicer laptop, but some people obviously will opt for no laptop and instead have an I-Phone or Blackberry. The choice is yours.

If the reader is right out of school and has a couple years of experience in the field, I would gauge the startup cost at $5,000 at a minimum. Having a good credit rating can help to finance a decent, working automobile. A base office is not required, as most of our business ideas are those that can be run out of a small apartment or garage and require no commercial renting or leasing.

License/Legal Requirements

Due to the very decent compensation and competitive nature of this type of business, the professional should have either a Microsoft or Cisco Network Professional Certification. Yes, there are plenty of existing consultants who were involved in this business before these professional certifications ever existed and so still have a devoted and loyal clientele as a result.

However, for you, if you are new, and/or young, and wish to break into this field, you must get clients, too. This means you will need to compete with people who are just as good as you are, but who do possess several certifications and some actual working experience, as well. So unless you are a master salesperson, which is usually not a trait of a good "techie," your ability to acquire clients will rely heavily on you being certified. Having certification could make or break your business when it comes to getting such clients.

Education/Experience

A four-year degree is not required, as most people can get the required skills via military training or in vocational schools. Due to the complex nature of this business, prior working experience and education are very helpful, and will help determine your success or failure. In the technology business, you can never stop learning. As technology progresses, so must your personal knowledge of it. Never rest on your laurels. Keep up, because the competition always does.

Detailed Notes

This is a very lucrative business, but one that often takes time to build. Ideally, this is for those who have strong experience in the respective consulting fields, either with networking or Microsoft technologies (preferably both), and who have adequate money and time to devote to building up a clientele.

You patience and efforts can pay off handsomely after a while, when getting clients is secondary to servicing them. The need for an advertising budget is also more pronounced than in other businesses outlined here. Despite this, be careful to use such a budget wisely.

Read my blog articles on advertising and promotions before you spend a dime. You are a small business serving other small businesses. You are a pillar of American capitalism. This should be emphasized in every step of this business. If you always conduct your business with the customer in mind, you will be very successful and happy.

Editor's Note

Specialties of this business may include the subfield of Computer Security Consulting. This consulting subfield may be attractive to those who have extensive experience with hacking and hacker-deterrent practices, as well as being able to retrieve lost data from hard disks. Hacking into Intel or Microsoft systems is rampant, as they dominate the computing base of the world. People indiscriminately browse the net, use dubious file sharing practices, and so get viruses. As they used to say in the old days--"if you lie down with dogs, you get up with fleas." People, however, will pay big money for lost data, children's pictures, etc., to have them retrieved by special skills and software.

How do you figure out what to charge? Well, I would start with an hourly wage of about $50.00 per hour. If your client has chores for you that require no more than ten hours of work a month and this is divided into two to three hours per week on average, then use this hourly wage to figure out a decent monthly compensation for a contract. Under no circumstance should you ever rely on a verbal contract, or just a handshake. As always, put such things in writing!

Chapter 3--Brick-And-Mortar Businesses

Home Daycare Operations

When it comes to stay-at-home moms looking for a way to bring in money, a home daycare often seems the practical solution. This allows the owner of such a business the ability to spend time taking care of their own child or children, while simultaneously earning money from taking care of other people's children. A mom/dad can spend the day organized around their child, as well as the children they are paid to watch.

This business is easily manipulated to fit a person's personal strengths. Specifics of the business decided by the owner, include things such as ages of the children, the number of days to be open or closed (including when to be closed for holidays), as well as the number of children they are willing to look after. These factors, along with the low startup costs, tend to make a home daycare very appealing.

Startup Costs

The amount you need to start a home daycare varies, depending on what type of supplies you already have. The initial investment will be for a business license, whatever permits are required by the state you live in, additional playground equipment, toys, and food. If you already own enough age-appropriate, outdoor, and indoor toys for the children you will be taking care of, then the cost is much less. Most daycare centers require parents to bring diapers, training pants, baby food and/or formula from home. Spare diapers may be a good purchase, in case of unexpected "emergencies." Additional costs may be incurred if your state requires daycare owners to be certified in First Aid and CPR, and/or if a certain type of insurance is required.

License Requirement

The requirement for a business license, and what type, varies according to your city and state. Along with local authorities, the National Child Care Information Center for your state can give thorough details about the type of business license, food license, or safety license that is required.

Education

There is no specific amount of education required in order to start a home daycare. You, of course, should have basic childcare skills. It is best if you have had prior experience in this with children of the age you want to take care of. However, if you are a new mom, then it is still perfectly acceptable to take in older children. If you have additional skills, such as a teaching degree, or experience in art, dance, or music, then these are definite advantages. This allows you to bring in a more particular type of clientele, and/or may give you a better chance of beating the competition in acquiring clients.

Environment/Daycare Setup

It is best to section off the home so that private areas are kept separate from daycare areas. After this is accomplished, the daycare area should be divided into work sections. There should be an eating area with highchairs, or kid-sized tables and chairs, if possible. For children that are not potty trained, there should be a changing table near the bathroom, if possible. A proper diaper disposal system should be used, a Diaper Genie, for example. A small, kid-sized table is optimal for the children to do crafts and activities. An area should be designated for reading, playing, puzzles, and such. The same area can be used for crafts, as long as the toys and activities have been put away.

The outside of the daycare should have items for kids to play on. This could be riding toys, a swing set, push toys, like a bubble mower, or something equivalent that makes noises, as well as soft and bouncy balls, durable plastic dump trucks, and possibly, even a sandbox. If so desired, the outside area can have a fence in order to aid in assuring the safety of the children. If a trampoline is available, a safety-net system must be attached.

Legal Paperwork

As a home daycare owner, you must remember to keep detailed records of each of the children. A form should be completed by a parent that includes all the important information. This includes complete names and addresses of parents, all phone numbers, such as home, work, and cell phone, any allergies the child may have, and a minimum of three emergency contacts that can be notified in case the parents cannot be reached.

For babies, a record must be kept of all diaper changes and feedings. This record must include the times and amounts for feedings. Some parents may ask you to keep track of the amount of wet and dirty diapers that their infant has. It is best to keep a binder or dry-erase board nearby, so that this information can be written or accessed quickly.

Details

The focuses for a successful home daycare are organization, safety, and child enjoyment.

Organization strongly affects how well your home daycare business will succeed. All items for play and education must have a place or a "home." Small containers for different categories of toys or games can aid with overall organization, and can help the children learn to put away the items on their own. Containers may be divided into cars, trains, blocks, books, board games, etc. The same method of organization can be applied to supplies that you use on a daily/weekly basis.

Having a daily and weekly schedule is a must if you want to run a successful daycare. Having numerous children around of various ages can be completely overwhelming if there is no organization of the daily and weekly routines. The easiest way to do this is to write out and post a schedule where it can be easily seen. Be sure to include times for meals, snacks, free play inside, educational play (like reading time, board games, or computer games for older kids), naps, and outside play, if the weather permits. Allow time for diaper changes, potty breaks (schedule these) and clean-up time between every change of activity. A weekly schedule may reflect small fieldtrips if the kids are at least of toddler age, or outdoor water play, again, if weather permits.

Safety proofing all parts of the daycare area is necessary. Basic baby/child proofing applies to every area. Each activity area should be wiped down between each activity. A simple, antibacterial wipe can come in handy to accomplish this quickly. All toys, games, and any other items the children come in contact with during the day, should be wiped down and cleaned with antibacterial cleaners on a daily basis. This is normally done at the end of the day. All counters and food preparation areas should be cleaned daily if not multiple times per day.

It is necessary to keep children safe, but it is also important to keep children entertained. Children are constantly learning and therefore must be challenged. This does not mean using flash cards all day. Babies can be put in swings with music and flashing lights, or placed in bouncy seats to get needed exercise. If they can sit up, surround them with several toys and soft balls. Older children learn through role-playing and hands on manipulation. Using a box full of clothing, along with various accessories, such as adult hats and shoes, is great for this type of play. Blocks, cars, plastic dinosaurs, dolls, wooden puzzles, board games, and toy kitchen sets are all standard play items that both boys and girls will love.

Other Important Details

Creating a menu for the meals provided to the children is necessary. Some states require a weekly/monthly menu to be on display for parents to review. Meals must be balanced and include protein, carbohydrates, and vegetables. Even if the state does not require one, the prewritten menu helps the business owner know what food to purchase and which items to cook for the day. The last decision you need to worry about during a busy day is what to cook to feed hungry children!

Marketing is important to get a home daycare up and running. Unlike a brick and mortar daycare center, a home daycare does not usually have road frontage drive-by advertising. You must put in the daily effort to bring in business. Depending on the number of children you expect to look after, marketing can be as simple as contacting friends and family to let new moms and dads know your daycare is open for business. This information can also be extended to your church or local schools.

In addition, some local stores, libraries, and city buildings, have bulletin boards for local residents to place flyers upon to announce their businesses or services. This is the perfect place to let those around you know that you are open for business. Make flyers with the basic information, such as the hours you are open, ages of children you accept, that references are available, etc. Be sure to include 'tear off tabs' with the phone number and your name on the bottom of the flyers.

One last thing to consider is having a backup plan. This is your business, but life will get in the way at times. Your child/spouse may become ill for a variety of reasons. You may become sick, or their may be a death in the family. These are not situations we want to think about, but you must consider what happens to the children in your care if one of these things occurs.

Find a qualified person who can take your place in case of an emergency. You may want to find a few different people, just as backups. This way, if your first backup falls through, there are still options. Be sure to notify parents of this backup plan from the beginning of their involvement with your business.

The last thing to remember is that keeping the parents informed is of the utmost importance. Make them aware of their child's progress, as well as any changes that arise in regards to schedule or tuition charges. A parent who finds out such information at the last minute is likely to be unhappy, and worse, will possibly begin searching for a new daycare provider.

Desktop Publishing

If you have ability for writing poetry, novels, or just about any other type of writing, Desktop Publishing may be a good business for you to consider. Whether you are going after consumers wanting to be published or just wish to publish free, public-domain books, this chapter may be interesting for all who are "bookish" and literarily inclined. As most writers find getting a bona fide agent or publisher is next to impossible, why not get around this by becoming a publisher yourself?

Startup Cost
There is only a limited requirement for startup dollars if you already own a computer. However, the direction and scope of your business will also affect the startup amount required. Usually, a computer and Internet access are a

prerequisite, along with software and office equipment needed for the business. As always, the biggest expense is in marketing and promotion. Remember to be careful how you use that marketing budget. If you do this, I would estimate approximately $2,000 as the necessary startup cost.

License/Legal Requirements

There are no license issues or legal requirements beyond proper accounting and taxation practices, but you will need to be aware of copyright law and the penalties that infringement of such could bring upon you. Be sure to get a clear handle on copyright laws and the concept of public domain. You should get some legal help in creating any contracts that you might be offering to your clients.

Education/Experience

Although you do not need any writing education to be a freelance writer, it does help. Even if you will not write yourself, aesthetic appreciation of what is good writing, and what would sell or become popular, will be required to know and succeed as a publisher. Education or aptitude of design, layout, and the ability to do book covers will also help. Further, if you have any artistic sense and/or an aptitude for the creative, it can help a long way in this business. Success will not happen overnight--good things usually take time. You will find out soon enough if you have an aptitude and the ability to be a good publisher. This is all that is required to get into this business.

Detailed Notes

New, independent, publishing houses are popping up

left and right. To different and various degrees, you will have to compete with them. Even if your books and genres are radically different from the myriads of other publishers out there, you will still compete with them for the attention of the reading public.

This means you will need patience if you are looking to be a publisher, because it can take months to get to the point where you have enough books to cover expenses and turn a profit, as well. If and when you attain this status, you are lucky, and the upside is that your residual income from books sales is now there for you, whether you choose to expand your repertoire of books or not. You can take a vacation and the royalties will still be there for you, if your books sell enough.

There are dozens of organizations and fairs geared towards publishers where you can seek to draw attention to your business, get group-based marketing powers, and find help if needed.

Freelance Writing

Freelance writing is often not only perceived of as a career that is incredibly difficult to enter, but difficult to make a living in, as well, and that used to be the case. However, the Internet has opened up a huge range of opportunities for those individuals looking to become a freelance writer. It is possible to write for magazines, newspapers, newsletters, websites, and any other number of publications and companies. If you love to write and have the necessary skills to be able to wow potential clients, then this can be an incredible career to embark upon, because there is nothing better than doing something you love for a living.

Startup Cost

The startup costs for those looking to get into the field of freelance writing are not as high as you may think. For example, you do not need to rent office space. Instead, you can set up an office at home. You will need to invest in a good computer, the relevant software (antivirus, office documents, and so forth), a desk, a printer, and other such equipment that may be necessary. You may already have some of this, and thus will minimize your initial costs. You can set up your office for around $1,000 but never invest in cheap equipment. You will need it to stand the test of time if you want to keep your overhead as low as possible, and for as long as possible.

License/Legal Requirements

There are no license issues or legal requirements beyond proper accounting and taxation practices, but again, you will need to be aware of copyright laws and the penalties that infringement upon these could bring. All work you do have to be original, or else you risk prosecution for plagiarism.

Education/Experience

Although you do not need any formal writing education to be a freelance writer, it does help. This is because many potential clients will ask to see a resume. However, there are some free competency tests available online, and they are always an excellent idea. Experience counts more, though, so you may find that you miss out on many high-paying jobs to begin with, and have to take low-paying jobs just to build up a little experience to your writing credit. You will have to learn how to write many different types of articles to ensure you can please all potential clients and fulfill all of their requirements.

Detailed Notes

The competition is fierce in the freelance writing industry and you may find you need to do it in addition to a main job for a little while, just to guarantee your income. This is because you do need to take a little time to build up a client list, and in the case of specialist freelance websites, feedback.

You will need patience if you are looking to be a freelance writer, because it can take months to land a lucrative contract. You cannot just apply for a job that pays $20 an article. Instead, you may have to write $2.00 articles, or place some on websites, like Associated Content free, just to build up a portfolio before you can go for higher-paying jobs. The latter is an excellent idea, anyway, because it will showcase your work and provide clients with example articles. Provided that you are dedicated to being a writer, you will find it can prove to be incredibly rewarding in the end.

Computer Programmer

A freelance Computer Programmer can be hired to build a specific piece of software for a business, or to contribute to the fixing of bugs in already existing software.

This type of business is suited only to those who already have the capability of building quality software, and should never be attempted by those without the knowledge and ability to program.

Startup Cost

The startup cost should be fairly minimal, assuming you already own a home computer. A website, domain name, and web hosting, is a necessity, as is a cell phone and business cards. Depending on the programming language that you develop in, a compiler and/or an Integrated Development Environment may be a significant cost, so you should always try to minimize your initial outlay by finding free alternatives to these.

Scheduling software and a word processor program is also important to your overall business, and so the costs of these should be factored into your startup costs. Getting some legal advice on your proposed contract/invoicing structure, and your tax status, is a good idea, as they wildly vary from one country to the next. Overall, startup costs may range from $300 to $1,000, depending upon the tools required for your particular language, lawyer fees, and web-hosting packages.

License Requirements

There are currently no license restrictions for a freelance Computer Programmer. As with any self-employed business, though, you should check your local tax and income laws.

Education/Experience

Although education is not specifically required, drawing up a list of your qualifications is a good way of legitimizing yourself in the eyes of potential clients. Specifically, a Bachelor's Degree in Computer Science, Computer Systems Engineering, or Software Engineering is really the bare minimum requirement for most programming jobs. This said, experience and ability are far more important in the eyes of potential clients. Providing links to your previous projects can help a great deal in attracting new customers. Contributing to, or developing an open source project is always a good idea, as it gives you a portfolio for clients and sharpens your own skills in the process.

Detailed Description

There are four main points to consider when deciding whether to become a freelancer. These are ability, management, dedication, and marketing.

Your ability to program well in several languages is a highly important factor. Many times, you will have to work upon a previously developed code base, and it helps if you can show that you are not only familiar with that language's nooks and crannies, but with the common development mistakes, as well. There will be many times that you will be hired to solve a certain problem, which can be done using a specific library or language construct. When you are developing the software yourself and determining language choice, you will need to allow for factors such as cross-compatibility, integration, and communication with existing software, and future development costs.

Programmers will often argue over the most profitable languages, but it is generally accepted that **C++, Java, Visual Basic 6**, and **VB.NET**, are all heavily used languages that will provide a steady income. A few freelancers also make very good livings translating applications written in old languages, such as COBOL, to new and more efficient ones. The amount of languages and libraries you can be productive in, directly affect your income and employability now.

Project management

Project management is a hugely important part of your freelancing life. **Gantt Charts** and **Work Breakdown Structures** are both highly valuable tools that allow you properly to manage your workload, and judge time estimations. One of the often-made mistakes with new freelancers is underestimating your current workload and the amount of time a job will take. **Microsoft Project** is pretty much the standard in this type of software, but there are some open source alternatives around, such as **Planner** and **OpenSched**. While scheduling tools will help somewhat, experience of similar work and honesty with the client, are valuable commodities in the business. Clients would much prefer an honest appraisal of timescale problems than a late product.

As part of any project management, good documentation is also useful to send to clients, to show organized and realistic project milestones, and including a good test plan. Not only does this all help maintain your professionalism, but also it is useful when it is time to visit your accountant (if applicable), and you need evidence of billable hours.

The two most popular methods of freelance programming are billable hours and a set fee. For the smaller "firefighting" projects, it is a good idea to bill for each hour worked, whereas a full build is usually at a set price.

One of the first points to consider is how valuable your time is. There are no real guidelines to what is considered cheap or expensive in this regard, as it differs from language to language, company to company, and person to person. A good research idea is to contact temporary recruitment agencies who employ programmers on short-term contracts, and ask how much you can expect to earn with your specific skills. It is commonplace when first starting your business to go quite a bit lower than these rates in an attempt to undercut the competition. Unless you already have an excellent reputation and good contacts, a cheap price will get you far, and most of your workload as a freelance programmer comes from repeat business.

It is imperative to your business that you find the middle ground between your greed and altruism. Performing a small task for a client may only take a few hours of your time, and presenting this on an invoice as non-billable, will increase the client's happiness towards you. However, your time is valuable and consistently performing free services will present you with financial problems later, and client expectations of prices you charge will fall dramatically. Your reputation now pays the bills, so it is highly important to be honest, approachable, and above all, reliable to your clients. You must do this without financially destroying yourself.

Lastly, any good freelancer needs to understand how to find potential clients and so must know the basics of marketing. Various books have been written on the subject of marketing, and it is worth it as an investment to get one of these.

Many programmers decide to have a 'pet project' on their website and to release it free. Although this is a small loss of income, it shows your capabilities in important parts of the business, such as GUI design, and correctness of product. In addition to this, it helps to legitimize your brand as a functional software house, while giving you the opportunity to keep your skills sharp. It is a good idea to release small programs you have built in the course of getting to know new languages or libraries. This "kills two birds with one stone," so to speak.

If the program becomes particularly well used, selling technical support, or adding a donation button, is another way of monetizing your work.

Communication and socially networking within the programming industry is a great way of picking up new clients. Nothing is better than getting a recommendation off somebody who already trusts you. This can be done through Internet forums, mailing lists, websites and **Usenet**--anywhere where there is a substantial community of users.

If it is financially feasible for you to do so, attend as many conferences as possible within your area of expertise, as this is a highly valuable networking opportunity. All of the major corporations and technologies hold annual or sometimes monthly conferences in which you can again sharpen your skills, and increase your client base. Visibility is key.

Several reverse-bidding websites can increase your income and client base. **Rent A Coder, oDesk,** and others can help to grow your business and provide a valuable alternative income stream, and as always, help to sharpen your skills.

General Tips:

- Never stop learning--Your income is now solely dependent on your skill set. If this becomes outdated, your potential streams of revenue disappear.
- Get legal advice--Whether this is concerning tax liabilities, contract disputes, or anything else, good legal advice is priceless.
- Be your brand--You need to present yourself as knowledgeable, confident, and assertive. If you see a problem with a stated requirement, voice your opinion. You are the expert there. Also, do not allow clients to bombard you with new requirements late in the project (although a little leeway is always nice).
- Use your time wisely--Your time is valuable to yourself and to others. In the beginning, instead of taking on a large project for a large sum, take on lots of little projects. You may earn less at first, but you will build a good range of clients who will come back to you again and again.
- Whether you like it or not, you are now a salesperson--The highest earning programmers in the freelancing trade are not necessarily the most talented, but tend to be the most marketable. Selling yourself is an art that many fail to master. If you can do this and have the skills to back it up, you are halfway to success.

Fundraiser

This business should appeal to those who like working with people, who enjoy helping people, as well as appealing to someone who enjoys a challenge. You need to be a well-organized person, someone who is self-disciplined and persistent. Like many businesses, you have to work through the knock-backs. However, there is no end of work available and you can create most, if not all of it, yourself.

Startup Cost

Depending on what you have already, there are virtually no startup costs. You should have telephone and Internet access and some space at home from which to work. A filing cabinet and desk could begin life as a milk crate and bench in your basement. If you use a cell phone with voice mail, you will not need an answering machine. For many fundraisers, there is little if any startup cost. Nevertheless, you could consider buying an established fundraising business. Obviously, there is the upfront purchase cost if you take this option.

License Requirement

There are two areas to consider here. One is you as an individual fundraiser, and the other is certain activities you might use to raise funds, e.g., running a raffle for example.

Be aware that each state has its own regulations. Running a raffle may require a license depending on whom the tickets are sold to. Contact your town hall or whatever local governmental department that deals with this issue. Get your facts right first, and once you know the ropes, future dealings will be straightforward.

Education/Experience

No formal education is required. Having some knowledge of the many ways funds are raised, and for which groups, will obviously help. You can become familiar with that in a few hours. You do not need experience and will quickly learn once you get started. Approaches to possible clients and fundraising activities that work are your two main areas of concern. You will quickly learn which ones work and which ones do not.

Detailed Notes

You must have a professional approach. You must present yourself as a professional. Having a great record of accomplishment is impossible for a beginner, so start small and achieve your goals. Obtain a reference from your first satisfied customer. Repeat the process with others. Use those testimonials to launch your fundraising business to the wider community.

There are two ways to generate income. You can charge a flat fee or take a percentage of the funds raised. Like so many other home-based businesses, you should work for a low fee initially, and once you are established--this can be in as little as a few weeks--your success will enable you to increase your fee.

The number of schools, kindergartens, sporting clubs, churches, hospitals, businesses, charities and the like, which rely on fundraising, is almost endless. Remember, you need to present as a professional person. Dress appropriately. A simple brochure you can create yourself, and deliver to local groups is a start. Word-of-mouth advertising is brilliant.

One of the best benefits of this type of work is the repeat business. When you do a good job of raising funds for a group, at the same time next year, have a guess as to whom they are going to call?

Repairperson Services

This business is easy to start if you love to fix and build things around the house. If your hobby is woodworking, fixing the plumbing, or dry walling, you could do this business with ease. There is competition and it is often brutal about pricing, but there is plenty of work to go around for a savvy self-starter.

Startup Cost
Repair Persons must have a truck and must use their own tools, business cell phone. An Internet website is a plus to begin with. Overall, the startup cost using used equipment can start at $5,000 dollars.

License Requirement
If the jobs taken are at or below $650 dollars, then there are no requirements for a contractor's license. Many people get around this rule by cutting up a job into segments that each limit the cost at around this price limit.

Education/Experience

There is no requirement for education, but experience and aptitude with anything that is related to home repair is a plus. We each have our own specialties, so take on jobs that you are good at, while learning and studying other various aspects of home repair.

Detailed Notes

The whole premise of contracting is to eventually hire and manage a couple of helpers or apprentices. Sadly, in the State of California, with the prohibitive Workmen Compensation laws and insurance requirements, this is now harder than ever. Contractors compete with repair-persons, and they usually lose work to them, usually because of pricing considerations.

One person's misfortune is an opportunity for another. A competent, hard working and reliable repairperson can always work, and be his or her own boss.

My friend is running this business with his wife and she clearly does a lot of work and helps him in his business.

Lawn Care or Landscaping

Starting a business in the lawn care industry can be a great decision. It has a relatively low startup cost, there is a market for the service virtually everywhere, and lawn care does not require special training or certifications. The great thing about this market is grass always grows, and people need to have it cut in the summer. During off-season, lawn care people collect leaves. As long as you are initially able to obtain customers, and you do a good job, you will retain them. They will continue to need their lawn cared for, and you will be the one they come to!

Startup Cost

If you plan to start a lawn cutting business, you do not need to invest a large amount of money. A typical lawn care startup will cost $2,000 or less. Obviously, this can vary, based on what services you plan to provide, and how much you are willing to invest. If you start out with the basic equipment, a lawn mower, edger, trimmer, basic yard tools, and a trailer to haul them in, you can plan to spend around $2,000. As your business grows, you can upgrade and add additional equipment. This will allow you to provide more services and perform them more efficiently.

License Requirement

There is no standard license required in order to provide lawn care service. You may start cutting lawns without any certification or license. While it is not required, it is a good idea to obtain a business license. Business licenses legitimize your business and give you exposure you would not normally have. Additionally, many commercial businesses, which can pay large dividends to your for lawn services, require you to have a business license before working for them.

Education/Experience

One great aspect of starting a lawn cutting business is it does not require any type of special training or experience.

If you are able to operate basic lawn care equipment, such as a mower or trimmer, you can perform lawn care. In addition, if you are considering starting a business in this field, you likely have experience mowing your own lawn, so you are already prepared!

Detailed Notes

Starting any type of business can be a stressful undertaking. As with any startup, it is important you sit down and plan a strategy before jumping in. Based on the amount of money you initially plan to invest, will help determine what services you can offer. Estimate the amount of time it will take to offer each service, taking into account the amount of time you can invest weekly to perform them. Based off that estimate, you should be able to determine a good base price to charge.

Typically, lawn care businesses have a minimum fee they will charge for mowing a yard. Starting from that amount, they will then scale the fee based on the size of the area. As mentioned above, obtaining commercial accounts can be a great boost to your bottom line. Companies usually pay more than residential accounts, and often have large areas that need maintaining. This means you spend more time working, and less time traveling between jobs.

In addition, while it is not required, basic advertising can really help you procure new accounts. This is especially important when starting out. Classified ads are a cheap way to reach many people through local newspapers and magazines. Placing signs on your work vehicles is also a great way to get exposure. A third, low-cost way to advertise, is by use of yard signs. Once you have a couple of clients, you can offer your service to them at a reduced priced in exchange for the placement of a small yard sign for your business in their yard. As long as you keep their yard looking good, people passing by will always notice the sign, and associate the great work done on it with your business name.

Party Planning

Being paid to party is a dream job that you can create for yourself! If you are the person who is always in charge of get-togethers, planning, and organizing the decorations, entertainment, and guest list, this could be a lucrative career for you. Great communication skills and creativity, along with excellent planning and budgeting abilities are keys to success in this business.

Party planners can either specialize in one kind of party, or take a broader approach and plan any sort of gathering. Planners oversee the entire party, and can be responsible for suggesting food, decorations, themes, entertainment, locations, caterers, and supplies. Good planners will know where to find all of the components needed and bring them all together.

Startup Cost

This is truly a business that can be started on a shoestring budget, and most people will already have the necessary equipment. A telephone with voicemail, Internet access, and a planning book are the only essential tools needed. You will also want to put together a party idea book, but the costs can be minimal for that, as well. Take pictures of parties you have planned to build a portfolio and show what you can do. A vehicle with decent storage space is helpful for transporting supplies and decorations as well.

License Requirement

You will want to register your business with your city, county, or state in order to get a business license. Start with your local government and ask what the requirements are for licensing, as they differ in each locality. You can also find out about tax laws at this point, as well. Get this information upfront and handle any needed requirements before you do anything else to avoid future problems with this.

Education and Experience

No formal education is required to start a party planning business. Experience, while not required either, can help. Planning numerous large parties, weddings, or reunions, can help you to get your feet wet and to learn the ropes. Engage your family and friends, and get some experience by planning their events for them free of charge. This way, you will gain experience while also building up your portfolio.

Detailed Notes

Like all self-employed business owners, Party Planners will have many duties:

- Marketing and advertising. In order to get business, Party Planners will need to market their services to those who might need it. This can be a broad stroke approach, or niche marketing to those you are most interested in working with. For instance, if you'd like to plan corporate parties, you might have flyers printed up advertising your services, and spend some time introducing yourself at all of the local office buildings. A website where you can add pictures and testimonials of successful events will be helpful if you also list your website address on your business cards.

- Proposals and Contracts. After you meet with the client and know what they are looking for, you will draw up a proposal detailing your services and charges, and both of you will agree to everything in a written contract.
- Food and beverage. Clients will want you to suggest and help pick out menus. Knowing what is appropriate for each type of event is imperative. Develop great relationships with caterers and other food vendors in the area, and always keep current menus handy.
- Locations. Research all of the party locations in your area, such as banquet halls, indoor and outdoor meeting places, and hotels. These are typical, but know about all of the "special" places in your area--museums, historical sites, town halls, sports stadiums, the beach--the possibilities are endless.
- Decorations. Your style sense will go a long way here. Get a general idea of the ambience that the client is looking for, and coordinate colors, flowers, and lighting to make it perfect.
- Invitations. Set up a system for handling the invitation process and RSVP's--perhaps using an online system. (Facebook Events or a similar system could be quite helpful.)
- Entertainment. Keep a good list of entertainers, such as bands, deejays, singers, even comedians and dancers. Ask people for recommendations and check them out on your own--you do not want any

surprises, since the entertainment can make or break the party.
- Vendors. Cultivate great working relationships with local vendors, like caterers, bartenders, party suppliers, location vendors, and more. Know which vendors are good and which are not, since you will be recommending these vendors to your client.
- Chief Money Maker. Here is the fun part! You will charge a fee to your clients for your work. You might charge an hourly rate, a flat fee, or a percentage of the total party budget, depending on what you feel comfortable with. Keep in mind that simple is best. During the contract phase, you will decide on your charges and negotiate them with the client. Typical charges are usually ten to twenty percent of the party budget, so if the party costs $5,000, you would charge between $500 and $1,000.

Editor's Note

Specializing in certain areas is beneficial. If you have casino experience and know casino dealers who might be available for moonlighting jobs, such as for fundraisers, i.e., Monte Carlo style events, you should pursue and specialize in this aspect of party planning.

Pet Care

For animal lovers, the pet care industry can be a great decision. It has a very low startup cost, there is a market for the service virtually everywhere, and pet care does not require special training or certifications. The great thing about this market is people travel, and they need help with their four-legged loved ones. As long as you are initially able to obtain customers, and you do a good job, you will retain them and grow your business by word of mouth.

Startup Cost

If you set your heart on starting a pet care business, you do not need to plan to invest a large amount of money. A typical pet care startup will cost $500 or less. Obviously, this can vary, based on what services you plan to provide, and how much you are willing to invest. If you start out offering only the basic services, pet sitting, dog walking, poop scooping, you do not even need to spend $500. As your business grows, you can upgrade and add additional equipment that allows you to provide more services, and perform them more efficiently.

License Requirement

There is no standard license required in order to provide pet care service. You may start walking dogs without any certification or license. While it is not required, it is a good idea to obtain a business license. Business licenses legitimize your business and give you exposure you would not normally have. Additionally, many affluent pet owners, who can be fussy as to whom they allow in their homes, will require bonding and/or insurance before working for them.

Education/Experience

A great aspect of starting a pet care business is that it does not require any type of special training or experience. If you have an affinity and experience with dogs and cats, you can perform pet care. In addition, if you are considering starting a business in this field, you likely already have experience with animals on your own, so you are already prepared! If you wish to gain experience, a part-time job in a pet store can be beneficial.

Detailed Notes

Each one of us is either a cat or a dog person. There is nothing wrong with learning about yourself and your preference first, before you embark on this new business. Armed with this self-knowledge, you can offer services that are more enjoyable and hardly seem like work to you, while charging good money for your services. Your customers will know you are passionate and dedicated in playing and walking with their dogs or cats.

Specialized fields in the pet caring business can be:
- Dog and cat grooming.
- Dog training.

Each pet-sitting business owner sets their own rate structure, which can vary greatly from other like businesses.

Most pet sitters charge a base rate per visit. According to United States nationwide polls conducted since 2004, the average per visit base rate for a half hour visit appears to be between $14.00 and $18.00 per visit.

You may have additional charges based on numbers of pets, mileage to and from your home, holidays, or tasks needed.

Private Investigator

A Private Investigator, or PI, is a person hired for investigations, usually by a private citizen. Private Investigators often work for attorneys in civil cases, or sometimes on behalf of a defense attorney. Many private detectives work for insurance companies to investigate suspicious claims. Some private investigators are hired to obtain proof of marital infidelity, or other illegal conduct, to help a client establish favorable grounds for a divorce. Collecting evidence of adultery or other "bad behavior" by spouses and partners is by far one of the most profitable activities licensed Private Investigators perform.

Startup Cost

While a Private Investigator can practice his craft from his home, it is advisable to have access to business office suites that are available per monthly charge of around $50.00. This affords even the novice investigator the illusion of having a successful practice, and professional environment. The business office suites give the renter a business telephone line, an answering service, and an office to conduct interviews with prospective clients. I would rate the startup cost of being a Private Investigator as low, being around $1,000.

Software Expense

Private Investigators use investigation software like **US Search, Net Detective, eDetective, Real-Time Spy**, and **Urgent Detective** to find people, conduct online background investigations, and search public records to find missing persons.

License/Legal Requirements

Many jurisdictions require Private Investigators to be licensed, and they may or may not allow them to carry firearms, depending on local laws and type of investigative work in which they specialize. Quite a few investigators are ex-law enforcement officers, but that is not a requirement. The craft of the trade can be learned while working as a security guard and so you can earn a living while taking the necessary classes.

Some states do not require a license specifically for private investigations, but they may require a business license, or have other legal requirements, such as training or certifications. Many states also require you to pass a test to become a licensed Private Investigator.

Following, is a state-by-state listing of contact information for obtaining your Private Investigator license.

Related Private Investigator Licensing Agencies:

- International Homicide Investigators Association.[1]
- National Association of Legal Investigators.[2]
- National Association of Criminal Defense Lawyers.[3]
- National Society of Professional Insurance Investigators.[4]

If you conduct business in more than one state, you may want to consider being licensed in all states that you

---

1 http://www.ihia.org/

2 http://www.nalionline.org/

3 http://ww.nacdl.org/public.nsf/freeform/publicwelcome?opendocument

4 http://www.nspii.com/

do business in.

Education

Educational requirements are important, as long as it relates to the law enforcement and security fields. Some of this education can be obtained in the military, and some of it is offered as adult education courses.

Detailed Notes

Investigators typically keep detailed notes during each case and often testify in court regarding their observations on behalf of their clients. Licensed Private Investigators take great care to remain within the law (e.g., being forbidden to trespass on private property, or break into homes) on pain of losing their licenses, as well as facing criminal charges. Irregular hours may also be required when performing surveillance work (e.g., outside a subject's house during the early hours of the morning).

Private Investigators also undertake a variety of work that is not usually associated with the industry in the public's view. For example, many Private Investigators are involved in process serving, the personal delivery of summons, subpoenas, and other legal documents to various parties involved in legal cases.

The tracking down of debtors can also be a large part of an Investigator's workload. When first starting out, it is advantageous to obtain work from a Private Investigation agency. Agencies usually specialize in a particular field of expertise. For example, some Private Investigation agencies deal only in skip tracing. Others may specialize in technical surveillance countermeasures, which is the locating and dealing with intrusive forms of electronic surveillance by competitors. As technology advances, so does the need for Private Investigators to increase their knowledge.

Modern Private Investigators prefer to be known as "Professional Investigators" rather than "Private Investigators" or "Private Detectives." This is in response to the negative image sometimes created by television shows or movies.

The United States Department of Labor, Bureau of Labor Statistics, published a useful article in the 2004-2005 edition of the **Occupational Outlook Handbook for Private Detectives and Investigators.**[5] The guide describes the nature of private investigation work, working conditions, qualifications, employment, training and advancement, earnings, job outlook, and related occupations. If you want to become a private detective, this is a great place to begin.

Repo Man

This business thrives in recessions and maintains an even course during normal times. Lenders can and will repossess cars, boats, and other vehicles when borrowers fail to make payments. You do not need to be a man--it is the name only, Repo Person would be more politically correct, but for a title, I just chose to stay conventional.

People with law enforcement or private investigation backgrounds should carefully explore this demanding and often dangerous business. It is highly recommended that

---

[5] http://www.bls.gov/oco/ocos157.htm

before you embark on this venue, you do some soul searching and see if this is indeed for you. If you are the adventurous type, and have confidently decided on this business, you might want to seek employment with an established repo agency. They often first send you out with an experienced agent, and this helps you to learn the ropes better and more quickly.

Startup Cost

The cost of doing this business is ongoing. You must find a car, boat, or other vehicle, and often at your own expense. Few agencies will pay expenses and cost of travel. A good, working vehicle is necessary. Some of the repo men operate a tow truck and the cost of leasing or purchasing one should be factored into the business expense of starting this venue.

License/Legal Requirements

In Florida and California, individual repo agents need to have a state license or work for an agency licensed by the state. Check your state of residence. In most states, this business is unregulated, but due to the flurry of repo activity and repossessions gone awry of late, Congress is looking at federal mandates to regulate this business, which currently exists rather like the Wild West.

Education/Experience

There is no formal schooling requirement for this business. Due to the availability of money and ease of entry, many convicts do this work after being released from the penitentiary.

Online courses are plentiful. Some in-house training is also available. Primarily, resourcefulness and ability of thinking on your feet will be required.

Detailed Notes

Some of the repo agencies are using high-tech methods to identify cars for repossession. The system is called MVTRAC, and it provides mobile digital cameras to repo companies to take pictures of license plates, as the repo men's tow truck goes down the road. The data is then matched to a list of licenses representing cars to be repossessed. When a match is found, the operator brings up additional info on the car to determine if he has spotted a wanted car. The agency gets about $200 to $400 as a repo fee from the car financing companies. This is shared with the independent repo person, and the amount is commensurate with his experience.

Marketing

Initially, getting business will be your least concern. If you work through the agencies, all you need to do is to accept the assignments. Later, when you gain experience, you might look into ways to market yourself, hence circumvent the agencies, and keep more of the money the end-client pays.

By this time, a website and listing in the Yellow Pages will be of help. You should always strive to grow and gain as much independence as possible in this field. Perseverance and hard work is the key. When you are already known in the community as an efficient, reliable, and safe repo agent, your assignments will be generated by word of mouth.

Advertising Specialty Business

If you enjoy advertising and gadgets, you might want to consider this business. It is very easy to launch and ideal to run from your home. Your clients will be other businesses--big or small, government agencies, or anyone who needs to establish a name and presence with the public. The gadgets are usually small items like books of matches, pens, or key chains that can be imprinted with a company, logo, and/or slogan. They are then given away, or made available in the offices of the purchasing businesses.

Startup Cost
Starting an Advertising Specialty Business is very cheap. Startup costs include a computer, a website, and some sample promotional goods.

License/Legal Requirements
There is a no license requirement for the Advertising Specialty Sales Professional. A business license will be required, as you are not the employee of the manufacturer (or importer) of the gadgets, you will be selling. Check your city or country for business requirements and costs.

Education/Experience
There is no specific educational experience necessary. However, a sales aptitude, people skills, and perseverance are a requirement for anyone considering this field.

Detailed Notes

There are a couple of important goals in establishing yourself in this business.

- Primary goal is to let people know of your new business. Get the word out.
- The second goal is to convince other business owners you can help them effectively and within budget to promote their businesses. Your demonstrated experience and advertising knowledge will increase as time goes by, and as you gain confidence and experience. You must, however, show creativity and fresh ideas from the first day.

Typically, Advertising Specialty Salespersons represent several companies, so they can offer a variety of personalized or printed products. When I first started in this business, I had only one company to represent, Kaeser and Blair, but as my business grew, I added others as demand grew, and as my clients asked for promotional items my original company did not have.

Marketing

Promoting this business will have to be as a two-pronged approach. First, in your community, you must drive around and hand out a catalog of your gadgets to likely businesses. Leave a business card and offer creative ideas for effectively promoting the prospect's business.

For example, if you trying to get a sports bar as a client, you might offer give-away coasters that have the basketball schedule printed on them, along with the name of the establishment. This must be ahead of the season's start in order to allow design and delivery of these items in a timely manner.

Secondly, in addition to your local business community, a website, search engine optimization, and web marketing, should all be included in your marketing and promotional agenda. I suggest joining the local Chamber of Commerce in your community.

Travel Agent

If you like to travel yourself, you might consider helping others with booking their hotels, airfare, or cruises. This business is very easy to get into and it does not require the level of training or sales experience that some of the other businesses require.

Startup Cost

Running a travel agency can start on a shoestring. It is a low-cost entry. A $500 to $1,000 startup investment is very often sufficient.

License/Legal Requirements

Check your state licensing requirements. My state, which is California, requires licensing that is maintained by the Insurance Commissioner. Yearly license fee is $46.00 per annum. Your state or country of residence might be different.

Education/Experience

If you are experienced by already having worked for a travel agent, you can skip this part. For those who are new to the travel industry, you can get training to ensure the successful launch of your travel agency and avoid common pitfalls. You might want to take an online training course or classes in your community.

Many host agencies offer free training when you sign on with them. The Outside Sales Support Network (OSSN) offers training information, as does the National Association of Commissioned Travel Agents (NACTA). People skills and professional conduct are more important than anything else for this business.

Detailed Notes

There are several methods of communicating with your client. These are the telephone, Internet (email), or face to face. For those who wish to start light and at home, the phone and email communication methods are preferred. Do keep in mind that while this business is competitive, exactly because of the ease of entry into it, your charm, personality, and professionalism, will determine if the client chooses you over the competition. This entails being available and accessible. Answer your phone and emails in a timely manner. If the client calls you at an inappropriate time, you can politely tell him/her to call back at another, more appropriate time.

Marketing

You would need to have a website, run some advertisements, and put up fliers, upon first launching your business. I rate the difficulty level of marketing this business as below average.

Editor's Note

If you want to have a leg-up on the competition, you can start by choosing a niche market. Try targeting just a specific country or continent. You can specialize in an age group, or method of travel, such as cruises, treks to the Himalayas, or deep-sea diving. You can begin with whatever you already have experience in, or an affinity for. This can make a whole world of difference. Of course, you can later expand to other lesser known (to you), but lucrative markets, as your success grows.

Dressmaker

If you know how to operate a sewing machine and enjoy the details of Dressmaking, you might want to explore this lucrative and easy-to-start business. This business is also called Custom Clothier, or Custom Dressmaker. Your task will be to sew garments for individual clients.

Startup Cost

Startup cost is quite considerable for this business. A well-lit room, a sewing machine, and basic sewing materials, are needed. Sewing machines can cost anywhere from $140 to $5,000, depending on the features they offer.

I highly recommend getting the best machine, but second-hand. You may also need a serger machine that allows you to create decorative and construction overlock stitches on all types and weights of fabrics. A serger machine can cost anywhere from $300 to $1,600.

Other things you will need are measuring tape, rulers, shearing and cutting scissors, pattern markers, needles and threads. You will also need a dress dummy and a full-length mirror to check on an individual garment in the making.

License/Legal Requirements

No special license is required other than the business license your local governmental jurisdiction might require.

Education

No special education is necessary other than some design and fabrics-oriented education.

Detailed Notes

There are several facets of this business and they are listed below:

- Weddings. The bridal business is a lucrative aspect of the sewing business. Many seamstresses make good livings just focusing on the creation of wedding gowns and wedding accessories.
- Home Decorating. Home decors and accents can also provide a big market for the home sewing business. You can specialize in sewing custom window treatments, including draperies, curtains, slipcovers, specially made pillows, shower curtains, bed covers, and other bedding materials.
- Alterations. Alterations can be a profitable business as many people have something in their closet needing repair, and they have no skills as to how to do it.
- Sewing for pets. This is a growing segment. You can create horse blankets, clothes for dogs, and other pets.

To enter successfully into this business, you will ideally have the sewing expertise for your chosen field, combined with an adequate general sewing knowledge. If you are focusing on draperies, you should know the best materials, the latest styles, and fabrics, to create the drapes your client desires. If you plan to start a bridal-gown, sewing business, you should know everything about wedding gowns.

Marketing

Word-of-mouth advertising is far the most effective way of spreading the word of a new sewing business. You do a good job for one client and the word gets around.

Other ways to advertise include posting on community boards, leaving your business cards and/or flyers in fabric shops, beauty salons, senior centers, and dry cleaners. Contact charity organizations and lend your sewing talents to charitable events. Also, get in touch with local performing groups that may require your services for any costumes or set designs. Visit craft fairs, so you will be able to network and meet potential clients.

You might want to establish partnership arrangements with your neighborhood cleaners. In the past, most cleaners kept an on-staff tailor, but now most of them collaborate with seamstresses for alterations. To collaborate with cleaners, you simply call around to find out who needs your services. When you work with a cleaner, you will need to set up regular times each week when they can have you in the shop, so customers who need alterations can meet you.

These are some sources where you can get more information about sewing as a Home Business:

mation about sewing as a Home Business:

- **Home Sewing Association,**
  http://www.sewing.org
- **American Sewing Guild,** http://www.asg.org
- **International Machine Collectors' Society,**
  http://www.ismacs.org
- **Professional Association of Custom Clothiers,**
  http://www.paccprofessionals.org
- **The Applique Society,**
  http://www.theappliquesociety.org
- **Smocking Arts Guild,** http://www.smocking.org
- http://www.hemmingaway.com

Expert Witness

If you have extensive experience in a field that can help determine court cases, such as medical professional, handwriting expert, or forensic scientist, you might want a second career as a self-employed expert witness.

Startup Cost

Starting up as an Expert Witness is almost at no cost. This statement is a bit misleading, as the cost of a college education, and continuing, professional education, is a considerable expense. There are online courses on how to build an expert business practice. If you have deep professional experience that is typically used in litigation, but unsure of how to go about the transition, you can spend the money to be trained. We do not think this is absolutely necessary, but it cannot hurt. The directories

listed in the marketing segment are member-only
(meaning you have to pay for them).

License/Legal Requirements

Licensing is not required for this business. However, depending on the area of your expertise, there are licensing associations available. The American Society of General Surgeons, and the American Council of Engineering Companies of Colorado, both have Expert Witness certification programs.

Education/Experience

You need to have extensive education and considerable work experience to become an "Expert Witness." In addition, you should possess the professional certifications your field has established and requires.

Police officers often serve as experts and they are trained in special programs for law enforcement officers, which are not available to the public, and often become "experts" simply by virtue of their completion of the courses, and the fact that the prosecutor has chosen to put them on the witness stand.

Detailed Notes

Expert witnesses can represent both sides of a legal case, plaintiff or defendant. As an Expert Witness, your task is to answer questions from both sides' attorneys, and to inform the jury of the appropriate technical aspects of the case.

Fields and areas of an Expert Witness are quite diverse. Some fields will keep you busy, while others are not in that high a demand. Here are some samples of fields and related work experiences. This list is incomplete and serves only as an example:

- Accidents and injuries (expertise in biomechanics, safety engineering, accident reconstruction, etc.).
- Business and Finance (accounting, forensic accounting, etc.).
- Computers and Technology (computer security, hacking, intellectual property, forensic computing).
- Human Resources (benefits, Human Resources related work experience).
- Medical (Medical malpractice, drug abuse, child abuse, etc.).

An Expert Witness would bill by the hour, but just like lawyers do, in addition, he/she will require and get a retainer, before they do any work. This is common practice. When there is a legal case, typically, it is the lawyer who finds and pays the expert. Sometimes, they refer to the client to do this. Most experts are not comfortable doing this, as it is an indication the case may be deemed weak by the lawyer, or somehow he/she just wants to finagle out from the responsibility of the fee. Do yourself a service; make sure you are paid before doing any work, such as depositions.

Marketing

Expert Witnesses typically are part of a consulting business. As part of this consultancy, they offer legal consulting as an Expert Witness. Law firms, government agencies, and companies (via their legal department) seek out and hire these consultants.

As an Expert Witness, you must network extensively with attorneys and other Expert Witnesses to get the word out about yourself, and your expertise. **Expertpages.com** website is a directory for expert witnesses. It is a membership only website, which means that there is a cost associated with joining.

Expertwitness.com is another online community whose stated purpose is efficiently to match experts with attorneys. Of course, there are other such websites. If you decide to join any, shop around first, ask questions (especially from your peers), before you spend a dime doing this.

There is a good book on the conduct of an Expert Witness written by Benjamin J. Cantor, who is a pioneer in the field of forensic photography. He has degrees in both law and engineering. His book's title is **The Role of the Expert Witness in a Court Trial (A Guide for the Expert Witness).**

Futures Broker

If you ever traded commodity futures, this business could be very interesting and profitable. With the currency and debt turmoil currently worldwide, many people started paying attention to real things, things that we use daily. Most of these goods are traded as commodity futures.

Briefly put, these are contracts to buy and sell a set amount of something (usually a larger quantity) at a future date. The prices of these change rapidly and these contracts are what commodity speculators exchange between each other. Additionally, large producers, called hedgers, are involved in the futures markets to lock into certain prices, hence insuring a given income for crops to be harvested, or livestock to be matured or slaughtered. The speculators and hedgers are the commodity broker's main clientele.

You can start a business as (what the industry calls) the Introducing Broker. You will need to sign up with a Clearing Broker also known as a FCM (Futures Commission Merchant) who maintains the trading operations, and has the membership seats on major exchanges worldwide.

Startup Cost

Running a futures brokerage from home is a medium-sized investment. You will likely need a home office, a computer system, a reliable Internet connection, a time stamp, a dedicated business phone line, and an 800 number. The costs of these are not great and most occur monthly. The initial cost is approximately $5,000, with a monthly overhead of $100 to $200. Some FCMs require the IB (Introducing Broker) to put up a deposit against any fines levied by the NFA (National Futures Association). This can increase the startup cost dramatically, but by no means should this discourage the aspirant.

Education/Experience

Having experience in commodities trading is very helpful to those who wish to explore this business. College education will also help, especially, if it includes finance and agricultural business curriculums. We believe that people should pursue their dream at all cost. Doing what you like and enjoying it throughout a lifetime, is the truest form of treasure. If being a commodity broker is your dream, but you have no experience, we suggest you get a commission-only job with an existing broker. They will mentor, provide training and help you get experience. Obtaining jobs in the industry is not hard, as most firms pay no salary or insurance.

Detailed Notes

There are several ways in which a broker can get new clients. Persuasive power, sales experience, professional demeanor and voice, coupled with deep knowledge of the business, are all essential. Most people who are not new to trading will work with a deep discount broker, but there are always those who need personalized service and advice. Getting and reporting fills, which are the time, date and price when the trade was commenced upon, is an essential part of this business, and a broker can make an active trader's life virtually trouble free. In the 1990s, most full commission brokers were charging in excess of $120 per round-turn.[6] Since about 2005, full-service rates have typically ranged between $30.00 and $80.00. Commission rates on futures contracts are paid per contract, not per order.

Marketing

You will need a professional website and should run

---

[6] Contrary to the commissions charged for stock transactions, commodities commissions are charged per complete buy/sell cycle__round turn.

ads in industry magazines, such as, **Stocks and Commodities, Futures**, etc., after launching your business. I rate the difficulty level of marking this business as above average.

Some IB's will offer leads (qualified prospects) to their brokers. The quality of these leads always depends on how they are generated. The best leads are people who have previously purchased related products, such as a book, or a course. Having these leads can help in opening new accounts and with the growths of your business.

Editor's Note

If you want to ensure your success as a commodities broker, you might want to start by choosing to become a specialist, such as a Spread Broker. Spread Brokers cater to a trader who usually simultaneously buys a long and short contract. In other words, one who buys and sells contracts in different maturity dates or in related products.

Shop around and you will find an FCM who you can have a decent clearing relationship. When I explored this business, I ran into a person, David Duty, who was CTA (Commodities Trading Advisor), and he was willing to allow me to set up shop under his IB business, as a satellite office.

The market exposure for such a trader is less and initial cost of entry, i.e., margin requirements, are lower. However, due to the complexity of execution, the demand for full service is emphasized. My book, **Commodity Trading 101,** explains in more detail what is involved in this business.

Manufacturer's Representative[7]

Are you an experienced sales professional who has been laid off? How would you like to travel to exotic Asian countries and have the opportunity to write off ALL the expenses? If you answered yes to the above questions, then you might want to consider moving up in the world and become an Independent Wholesale Representative.

Manufacturers often hire an outside, independent, sales force to represent their various widgets to stores and end-users. Most people starting out as Independent Sales Representatives have several years of sales experience and are thoroughly familiar with their respective product line. Example of product lines can be found by researching MANA[8] or any of the trade associations for individual industries, ranging from house ware, to food service.

Startup Cost

If your manufacturer base is mainly in Asia, as most representatives today prefer for obvious cost considerations, then business trips to these clients are often necessary. Seeing the factory and meeting the people there will put your mind at ease, and create confidence in your marketing. The startup cost for this business I would rate

---

7 Sometimes also called as independent sales rep

8 Manufacturer's Agents National Association
http://www.manaonline.org/

as rather high for this and other obvious reasons. Big sales may take time. In addition, visiting trade shows is necessary and that will be an initial expense.

License/Legal Requirements

There is no licensing requirement for this business.

Education/Experience

A four-year degree is not required, but highly recommended. Many manufacturers will not talk to you, unless as a newcomer, you have a degree, or unless, of course, you have demonstrated experience with their competitors.

Sales experience and aptitude are more important than anything else for this highly lucrative, yet demanding business. As with all our businesses described in this Blog, previous experience in the field is highly recommended.

Detailed Notes

The business model for this field has not changed. It is far more cost effective with better sales penetration to hire outside experts to sell your wares in volume than to keep and maintain an in-house sales force. The independent representatives often have contacts and a knowledge base that is invaluable to the long-term relationship the manufacturer wants. Recently, manufacturer's representatives have been known to also train in-house sales staff on products, and sometimes they even make joint sales calls.

Read my articles on advertising and promotions before you spend a dime. You are a small business serving other small businesses.

Editor's Note

There are other ways, often with lesser barriers and lower costs, to break into this business. This is wholesale for online entities such as eBay or Amazon. The moneymaking potential is there. Many people, including semi-retired manufacturers' representatives, do this part time with great monetary rewards. Some smaller manufacturers want to sell to anyone wholesale who is willing to buy and warehouse their goods. All you have to do is to pay for it, and they will deliver.

Sometimes, the offer is too good to be true, where the manufacturer offers to sell individual items and then even offer to drop-ship to addresses you specify.

I tell my readers to verify these businesses carefully, as, again, the offer seems too good to be true. Selling on Amazon, eBay, or some other venue is sometimes found under the business category of import/export businesses.

Webmaster

If you are an Internet aficionado with extensive web programming experience, you might want to consider this business. A Webmaster is a designer, organizer of website code and images. Typically, his clients are individuals or small companies who cannot afford a fulltime Webmaster on staff. Recently, with the advent of template-based websites, a Webmaster is more of an organizer of webpages than a designer of a new website. However, there are Webmasters who are expert graphics designers/artists and who will design custom websites from scratch.

Startup Cost

The cost of setting up a freelance Webmaster business is low. If you do not own a good computer or have fast Internet access, then you must obtain those. The overall setup cost of this business is under a $1,000.

License/Legal Requirements

No special license is required other than the business license that your local governmental jurisdiction might require.

Education

As a Webmaster, you are expected to be well versed in Internet technologies, XML, HTML, PHP, JavaScript, Perl and database technologies. This, you can lean by doing, or from formal training, such as an Associate Degree program for Webmasters. However, this is not necessary to be in the business. More important, is the full understanding of how text, graphics images, and streaming video/audio integrate on a webpage. This comes from related work experience.

Detailed Notes

To enter successfully into this business, you will ideally have either working experience as a Webmaster for a company, or have demonstrated skill and experience for several websites that you have built either for profit, or as a non-profit venue. A freelance Webmaster, besides a resume, can typically show a portfolio of designs and webpages maintained in the past.

A good Webmaster will also help with monetizing the client's webpage, by having affiliate programs or other pay-for-click partners. He/she will have an expansive knowledge of Internet marketing and would be able to suggest options to clients. Some Webmasters are specialists in SEO technologies, automated, database-backed, content, management systems, such as Word Press.

Marketing

Internet is the most effective venue to advertise you and your craft as a freelance Webmaster. Many Webmasters write and publish code, and maintain professional relationships with their peers via forums and blogs. A very professional and interactive website with a blog would be a start to anyone wishing to build a client base.

You might want to establish partnership arrangements with small Internet hosting companies and computer user groups. Template design is also a venue where you can give away a nice website template in hopes that custom work and business contacts would later follow.

Traditional printed media advertising is best with your FREE local independent newspaper for this type of business. Again, they are free, and their main source of revenue is advertising. While this business can be easily conducted over the phone, long distance, it is very useful to cultivate and maintain local contacts in your community. Some people need to see their clients/partners face to face.

Resources for webmasters:

- http://www.webmasterized.com/
- http://www.talkfreelance.com/
- http://www.code4gold.com/
- http://wordpress.org/
- http://aboutawebmaster.com/

Antiques Dealer

If you love and know about antique furniture, old heirlooms, and knickknacks, then this business might just work for you. An Antique Dealer would buy at private sales and auctions, and then resell in a shop that is typically operated as a co-op to save costs. Later, if successful, the dealer might open his own shop, but many dealers are content to work in a co-op. In addition, recently with the advent of the Internet, some antiques dealers prefer to conduct their businesses online.

Startup Cost

Antiques dealers have setup costs that include their

inventory. This alone can initially cost several thousands of dollars and profit is never a guarantee. This business is not without expenses or risks. In addition, the dealer might have to refurbish and improve the furniture he bought at the auction if there are minor scratches, and wear and tear. To save expenses, the dealer often chooses to perform these tasks himself. It is important to note that that any work preformed on an antique piece must be performed expertly or it would lower the value of the item. To move furniture and heavier items, the antique dealer should have access to a truck.

License/Legal Requirements

There is no licensing requirement for this business other than a resale license and a business permit. A dealer buys at auction, but sells retail, so to collect sales taxes (where applicable), is incumbent upon them. Of course, in states were sales tax is non-existent, this chore is avoided.

Education/Experience

It takes some experience to know the value of good antiques. Some people have been buying and selling antiques as a hobby, and they have been around old and more expensive things throughout their lives. To them, this business would come naturally.

Detailed Notes

There are many kinds of dealers in the trade. Some are fulltime. Some are doing this as just a hobby, or for social reasons, and/or maybe for tax purposes. The tax advantages of traveling to sell and buy are enormous. A perceptive Antiques Dealer can literally travel throughout Europe, buying and writing off all the expenses. One can spend the winter in the Southern United States, selling, and write off the expenses.

With paper money getting worth less and less, and many people realizing this, they choose to put a considerable amount of their disposable income into antiques. They then save these for their retirement years, at which time some of them will sell only when they need a little extra cash. Some retired people turn into fulltime Antique Dealers. It is helpful to sit down and write out the reasons you are attracted to this business, and to decide what type of a dealer you wish to become.

Marketing

Antiques Dealers typically sell on antiques shows and from inventories displayed in co-op antiques shops in tourist towns such as in Petaluma, California.

Nowadays, the Internet plays a big part of keeping in touch with peers, displaying inventory, and even transacting business.

In order to be in a co-op shop, the dealer must pay for an area where he can display his antiques and in addition, he also must work in the store. He will have to sell other dealers' inventory when they are not present, and so fellow dealers will sell his.

Gift Basket Sales

The gift baskets business is a multi-million dollar industry. Baskets can be sold to individuals, to businesses, and for fundraisers. They are a gift item with a little personal touch that people are willing to pay extra for.

Giving gift baskets is commonplace these days. To start well, you will need a familiar market. If you know people in the real estate business, then you can specialize in housewarming gift baskets, since some realtors offer these at closings to clients, hoping to gain valuable referrals. Ideally, you can specialize in baskets for certain occasions or a particular clientele. Whatever venue you take, do your homework. It is a good plan for this but in general, all other businesses embarked on, finding gift basket creators in the area, and study them. Use the result as a guide for your business plan.

Startup Costs

Your initial costs can be as high as $2,000 to $5,000 with supplies, costs of advertising, and equipment. A computer and Internet access, business phone, fax, printer, and necessary software will be needed for bookkeeping and inventory tracking.

License Requirement

Any foodstuffs kept in your home for resale may require a sanitation inspection or a special license. Check your governmental jurisdiction before moving forward and deciding what kind of baskets you will make. Offering baskets with alcohol is generally illegal without a liquor license. Before you start your business, make sure that all of the proper paperwork has been filed and all licenses obtained.

Education/Experience

Making gift baskets requires creative thinking and skillful design, along with a talent for crafts. Professional presentation skills and a demonstrated ability to close a business deal are also a strong advantage to those who are thinking of entering this lucrative, home-based business.

Detailed Notes

It is advisable to offer gift baskets that range in size. This way you would attract potential customers across all income levels. If you offer something for everyone, your business will naturally grow. After you have managed designing a line of baskets, take photos and create a nice catalogue of them. This way, you are able to advertise your craft. You might want to offer custom-made baskets at client request.

Selling gift baskets is based on themes and seasonal events. These are just some of the themes[9] from the website of Internet based, **moms.com**.

Baby shower	Golf	Get Well
Pet owners	Graduation	New Home
New Moms	Mother's Day	Baptism
Christmas	Father's Day	Chocolate Lover's
Easter	Birthday	Pasta Lovers
Valentine's Day	Wedding	Divorce

---

[9] http://www.Internetbasedmoms.com/ideas/gift-basket-ideas.html

Used Car Business

If you have good work experience as a mechanic, you might enjoy this multifaceted business. Buying used cars and fixing them is an old business, which has recently enjoyed resurgence with the adding of such things as kits for biodiesel, and other fuel-saving alterations.

Startup Cost

To get into this business, you should have ample parking spaces and a garage at your home. With the tools and equipment, this business is not without a hefty startup cost. You can get around the professional garage requirement by renting garage space with a professional, under-the-ground crawlspace in order to work on the underside of a car. If you do not have the funds to repair at home, you can still do this business by only buying wholesale and never touching the cars, other than detailing them.

License/Legal Requirements

Getting a dealer's plate is advisable, but not mandatory. You can buy, modify, and resell a used car without being a used car dealer. However, to buy at auctions reserved to dealers, you should own a dealer's plate. In addition to this, most states limit the number of times you can transact cars in a given time span; i.e., exchange auto titles as a private party. If you exceed the limit, they either disallow it or even deem it a misdemeanor offense and will fine you. States are broke right now, so they will look at any way to raise revenue.

To find details on how to obtain dealer plates, you should contact your State Department of Motor Vehicles, or your country's jurisdictional agency in this matter.

In California, if you wish to transact less than 25 cars per year, a $10,000 surety bond is required; otherwise, the bond amount must be $50,000. Do not get discouraged. You do not need to put up this amount. A bond is like insurance. You must pay a premium to obtain this bond and the cost depends on your credit rating. Check the requirements of your residence locale to determine what is needed.

If getting your own dealer's license is too much for you, check around your area. You might be able to collaborate up with an existing dealer and rent their dealer plates, which you can use to purchase cars wholesale and at closed auctions.

Education

In order to get into this business, you should know as much as possible about mechanics, and body repair. You should be well versed in all aspects of motor vehicles, such as the engines and auto parts. You should do this either as a hobbyist, or as a professionally trained mechanic. Your level of knowledge about cars will determine what aspects of this trade you can successfully pursue.

In some states, like California, all vehicle dealer applicants must take a mandatory six-hour course of training as mandated by the DMV (Department of Motor Vehicles), before obtaining a vehicle dealer license. They must pass a test at the DMV.

Details

Several aspects of this business are interesting and possibly very lucrative. Many used-car professionals specialize in car makes such as BMW or Mercedes. There are several reasons for this. If you are trained in German cars, you are a specialist, and it may not be as easy for you to work on other vehicles. German cars are well built and have a good resale value. In addition, they have owner prestige to them, even as used, older models.

An acquaintance of mine had purchased a 1980 Mercedes 240 TD in good running condition with around 140,000 miles for the price of $2,500. She had the car converted to biodiesel. Any diesel engine can be converted as long as there are no rubber seals used in the fuel system. Since vegetable oil is a strong solvent, the rubber seals can be damaged.

Marketing

Word-of-mouth advertising is far the most effective way of spreading the word on a new mechanic or a dealer. You do a good job for one client and the word gets around. Advertising of vehicles can be done very effectively online, by using eBay or your very own website. Social networking media can also be used very effectively.

As a used car professional, you might choose to work on cars for friends and acquaintances in addition to reselling some. Most used car dealers who operate from home are doing just that. A good, honest reputable mechanic will never have to worry about putting food on the table.

Window Cleaner

This is about the simplest business to get into. All you need is initiative, good health, and good people skills. Window cleaners work strip malls, office buildings, and other structures. They nicely approach business owners and ask them if their windows need cleaning. A good idea is to offer a free cleaning initially, to show good faith, and prove good intentions. Many businesses consider these offers intrusive, so you must have very good people skills and perseverance in order to flourish and survive this easy, yet competitive business.

Startup Cost

Startup cost is almost non-existent for this business. Besides supplies and equipment, you hardly need have any running costs. A cell phone and a good working truck is also a necessity, but many people already have these. You will need standard washing equipment (e.g., bucket, brushes, cleaning detergent), and some larger window cleaners are now using more expensive pressurized water systems. (See note below.)

Business cards and promotional side banners on the truck are an advantage. I estimate this business can be launched under $1,000 if you already have access to some of above-listed necessities. If you start completely fresh, out of high school, you can get all you need for $5,000 or less.

License/Legal Requirements

No special license is required other than the business license that your local governmental jurisdiction might require. However, if you choose to work on tall structures, you might need a certificate in safe rope access and abseiling

Education

No special education is necessary other than some good people skills and a professional demeanor. I highly recommend kids in high school who are willing to learn the craft of hard work and entrepreneurship, to do this part time; everybody is willing to give a shot to a high school kid. This way, when you finish school, you already have a route to make extra cash.

Marketing

Word-of-mouth advertising is far the most effective way of spreading the word on a window business. You do a good job for one client and the word gets around.

Editor's Note

Alternatively, if you do not like windows or find window cleaning too competitive and low profit, you might consider getting a pressure washer at **Costco** or from some other discount store. If your residence is near a marina, you can approach boat owners for pressure washing their boats when it is dry-docked. Some people can get a $100 to wash a larger boat. Obviously, boat owners are in a higher income bracket than some small business owner with a storefront. Try to see what works for you.

Cleaning Business

While the janitorial business is typically about cleaning office buildings, it is also a close relative of a home cleaner, who practically does the same thing--cleaning the premises. Because of the close similarity, this chapter will cover both residential and office cleaning. To be in the cleaning business you must be insured and bonded. Shop around to find the cheapest insurance and bonding, otherwise nobody will let you into their homes or office buildings.

Startup Cost

You will need to invest in a very good quality vacuum cleaner, a mop, and some rags. You can purchase old t-shirts for dusting, and use towels for heavy-duty cleaning. You can wholesale-purchase cleaning liquids. Alternatively, you can become a green business, by using only natural substances like vinegar and water solutions that tackle almost any cleaning jobs. If you do residential cleaning, the woman of the house might be very particular, supply the cleaning materials herself, and specify exactly what to use. At any rate, this is an inexpensive startup business. Reliable transportation and a website are needed for projecting a professional image. Business cards should also be made and given out liberally. Startup cost for this business can be under a $1,000.

License/Legal Requirements

No special license is required other than the business license that your local governmental jurisdiction might require. However, as the new trend, the International Janitorial Cleaning Services Association offers a certification program that is relatively inexpensive to get. This might not only increase your knowledge of more efficient cleaning techniques, but will give your cleaning business a degree of legitimacy. If you always wanted to tell your friends about having a green business, you can obtain a certification through the Green Clean Institute. If you wish to specialize in repair and restoration of carpets, you should get a stain removal or restoration certification through the Institute of Inspection, Cleaning and Restoration.

Education

No special education is necessary other than some good people skills and professional demeanor.

Details

It is well advised to limit your service area. When first starting out, select one area upon which to focus. Driving back and forth across the country will cost you both time and money. For example, you could start your janitorial service within a 20-mile radius of your home. Offer deep discounts to get started. Offer a new customer rate that will get you in the door and then do such an amazing job, that the client would be foolish not to use your regular bi-weekly services.

Marketing

Word-of-mouth advertising is far the most effective way of spreading the word on a new cleaning business. You do a good job for one client and the word gets around. Collaborate with complementary businesses and offer their customers discounts. Carpet installers, independent commercial real estate agents, and pool-servicing companies, are just a few of the possible partners for a janitorial service.

You can start a customer referral campaign by offering discounts for existing customers who refer new business to you.

Carpet Cleaning

Carpet Cleaning is a specialized cleaning service, a $3.3 billion industry. You often see a carpet cleaner in apartment buildings after a tenant vacated the premises. Usually, after minor repairs, they are the first people to call. You can see their van with the specialized, steam-cleaning equipment inside, and the large tubes running up to the apartment needing to be cleaned. The large tubes carry the warm water with detergents to do the cleaning via hot water extraction.

Startup Cost

You will need to invest in very good quality steam-cleaning equipment, and a van or a truck. You can purchase used, heavy duty, carpet-cleaning equipment mounted on a truck or a van, already equipped from a person who is leaving the business. Alternatively, if you do not have the startup capital, you can rent these weekly, monthly, or even daily, hence giving you the opportunity to try this business. Once you show profit and start liking this business, you can invest in the equipment for yourself. If you wish to purchase the equipment, the startup cost would be perhaps as high as $40,000 (including a used van).[10]

License/Legal Requirements

No special license is required other than the business license that your local governmental jurisdiction might require. You could get a stain removal or restoration certification through the Institute of Inspection, Cleaning and Restoration.

Insurance and bonding is essential in this business, especially, if you wish to get commercial clients, such as apartment buildings or offices.

Education

No special education is necessary other than some good people skills and professional demeanor.

Details

There are two basic types of truck-mount, carpet-cleaning machines; one is a slide-in unit, and the other is van driven. The slide-in truck mount can be moved from one vehicle to another, and runs on its own engine, but it takes up more space. The van-mounted truck mount is one unit, and runs off the engine of the van. The van-mounted truck mount takes up less space, but is more expensive than a slide-in, truck mount carpet cleaner.

Before you decide to buy a truck-mount carpet cleaner, you will need to:

- Compare the new and used truck mount carpet

---

[10] http://www.jondon.com/used/index.php

cleaning machines.[11]

- Determine if you want van-mounted or slide-in carpet cleaning machines.
- Make sure all used carpet-cleaning equipment is included when buying used equipment from a private party.
- See if financing or leasing is available on the truck-mount carpet cleaners for sale.
- You should look into the Steambrite financing programs. Get an online quote for leased equipment.

It is well advised to pay cash when you buy a truck-mounted carpet cleaner, if it is possible. If you have money, you can always haggle over the price. Do not pay in actual cash, however. Pay for the truck mount with a cashier's check or bank draft, so you have a record of payment. Further, consider leasing the carpet cleaning equipment from a reputable leasing company. The advantage of leased equipment is that it is maintained on a frequent and regular basis.

Marketing

Tell everybody about your new business. Offer specials to new clients and anyone who makes referral to you. Have a side and back banner on your truck or van with your business name, telephone number, and webpage.

Makes and models of truck-mounted, heavy-duty, carpet-cleaning equipment:

HydraMaster BobCat 3.0. BobCat 3.5. Aquacat 3.5. Pro-

---

[11] http://www.hydramaster.com/inside/articles/article3.asp

fire 3.7. Profire 4.2. Spitfire 3.2. Spitfire 4.0. Boxxer 318. Boxxer 421. Boxxer 427. Maxx 450. Maxx 450D. Maxx 470. CDS 4.2. CDS 4.4. CDS 4.6. CDS 4.7. CDS 4.8. Crossfire 3.7. Crossfire 4.2. Crossfire 4.4. Hydracat. Titan.

Prochem Bruin 1. Bruin 2. Cub. Cub XL. Bear. Bear Cat. Blazer. Blazer XL. Trail Blazer. Legend. Legend SE. Legend XL. Performer. Performer 405. Performer 805. Peak. Apex. Everest. Hydraulic direct drive. PTO.

Powerclean Liquafire 445 with 22 hp Kawasaki. Liberty XT. Victory 45 and 47 with Kawasaki 27 hp. Victory 45 and 47 with Kohler 31 hp. Freedom XT. Genesis 56 and 59 with 52 hp Ford. Genesis 56 and 59 with 49 hp Nissan. Genesis 59 with Hyundai 68 hp. Genesis 59 diesel with 52 hp Isuzu. Genesis DXT. Genesis 59 ZXT.

Steamway Powermatic Legacy 1100. Powermatic Legacy 1150. Powermatic Legacy 2100. Powermatic Legacy 4100. Powermatic Legacy 4200. Mastermatic 4000. Mastermatic 4200. Equinox 7200. Omega. SUX Lt. TURBOMATIC. Supercube 33, 36, 45. 9100lx. SHX 5600.

White-Magic Commander. Commander HO. Triton GS. Triton LS. Triton DS. Rebel.

World of Clean Cleanmax 1836. Cleanmax FX1836. Cleanmax 2545. Cleanmax FX2545. Cleanmax 3047. Cleanmax FX3047.

Cross American Second Generation Super Charged Recoil 3 XPS System. Kwik Steam and Next Generation Power Booster. Second Generation Super Charged Scorpion 3 XPS System.

PART TWO--Operating your Business

Chapter 4--Marketing

No matter what you choose to do as a business, it will not be successful unless you effectively market it. Marketing is more of an art than a science. Every business needs a custom-tailored marketing plan, and these might be different for a bookkeeper, as opposed to a person starting a landscaping and law maintenance business. However, some of the ideas and venues will be similar, as all businesses must take similar steps to announce their new venture. This includes telling friends and family. If you are a member of a church or other community organization, you should make an announcement there, too.

Each and every business has a unique sphere of existence, a peer network of similar enterprises. Often, this is where the main source of the revenue will come from.

As a publisher, I make most of my money working with **Amazon.com**. This is not a surprise, as they are the largest online bookseller. Learning to use this business sphere is unique to every business. For example, a pet care business will be wise to learn the best way to work with veterinarians, pet stores, and other businesses that could make referrals.

The best marketing ideas and advertising venues are often free. I cannot impress the reader enough about the importance of this. You can spend a ton of money for expensive PR and magazine ads, but ignore the obvious and free idea for your business. As small entrepreneurs, you must think outside the box.

A savvy businessperson will test all marketing venues with as little capital outlay as possible, after each test try, he must measure for tangible results which are obviously sales.

If something works, use it, but if it fails then you must move on, and try something different.

This chapter might be colored by my perspective as a marketing person for books, as I am in the business of publishing. Do not let this dissuade you from using common sense, the wisdom, and experience of your peers. Try others things that might work for your chosen business.

Running a profitable business is a three-facetted endeavor, which I can demonstrate as a triangle.

1. Product/Service development;
2. Advertising/Promotions; and
3. Sales/Marketing.

These three facets act like the legs of a three-legged stool[12]; afford stability for the least cost. When you have these three areas in balance for your business, you will be on the right track.

---

[12] To find out if this is true, check the math forum on this subject, http://mathforum.org/library/drmath/view/53267.html

Off-line or Brick and Mortar Marketing

- Mailing list rental
- Postcard mailing
- Letter mailing
- Magazine or newspaper ads
- eZine ads

Internet Marketing

- Website setup (domain name registration, SEO, websites submission)
- Online lead generation
- **Google AdSense** and **AdWords**
- Partnering with other websites

Regardless of what kind of a marketing plan you choose, ideally you should do both (offline and online). You will be required to present a sales copy to your prospects.

Writing an effective sales copy

How well you write the ad or sales copy for your product or service will ultimately determine if people are going to order it or not. An effective ad copy has a headline-- must be eye catching and unique, have bulleted points to outline the fine details of your proposition, and have testimonials at the end. Make sure you have testimonials, *even if it costs you some free service or samples of your product.*

Practical Advice for Effective Copy Writing

I strongly recommend you hiring freelance professionals to write your ad copy. If you are short of funds, you might look at your competitor's websites, magazine ads, or fliers. Study them; use those you know to draw business. Find ideas from their success. Eventually, you will be able to write effective ad copies, but it will take time and lots of practice--trial and error.

Traditional Off-Line Marketing

Sometimes, this is called direct marketing. Effective marketing is a combination of three factors represented in percentages of importance:

1. The quality of your product or service - 25%,
2. The effectiveness and quality of your ads - 50%,
3. Your audience - 25%.

This may seem different from what you have imagined, but trust me--this is true. **Coke** runs ads against **Pepsi**, seemingly offering the same product to the public who can also drink dozens of other soft drinks.

Of course, **Coke** does not use the concept of direct marketing but they are spending ad dollars keeping the above percentages in mind. This does not mean you should have an inferior product or service--far from it--this means, however, the best product will not save a business that operates in a vacuum, i.e., one nobody knows about.

Let us look at the different off-line mediums one can choose from:

- Classified Ads
- Display Ads
- Full-page Ads

- Direct Mail Letters
- Direct Mail Postcards
- Fax Blasting
- TV/Radio Infomercials

Classified Ads

This is a cost effective way to put the word out for your products or services. When choosing the magazine or newspaper, remember that it should be in line with the genre of your services and/or product for the demographics and budget of the readership you are targeting. For example, a dog-grooming service would be smart to take out a small classified ad in a pet magazine. The cost of the ad will depend on the number of subscribers and the size of the general readership of the paper or magazine.

The **USA Today** has a Sunday edition and depending on your market, placing ads in the classified section there may work. Check the classifieds and see if a similar business to yours has an ad there. Periodically, you should check back with the paper. If you see a competitor who, week after week, is advertising there, then you know that it is working, and this is a green light to you to take it a step farther and check advertising prices with the paper.

Mailing List Resources

When embarking on a mailing campaign, whether it is the postcard or letter kind, it is imperative to obtain a mailing list that is fresh, targeted to your audience, and cost effective. The source for obtaining a mailing list is the *Standard Rate & Data Service*, but everybody knows it only as "SRDS." A few pointers on using the SRDS effectively;

- You always rent a list and never purchase it.
- It is advisable to test any list with its smallest quantity, and if it proves to be profitable, then purchase more.
- You should make sure your ad copy is as perfect as possible, because, no matter how good your list is, if your ad pitch is riddled with typos or poorly constructed, nobody will take it seriously, let alone purchase from you.
- If time permits, do the mailing yourself. Alternatively, you can hire mailing houses that will do this task for you, for a fee, of course.
- Stay away from lists that are results of opt-ins from **Entrepreneur, MLM,** and other business-opportunity magazines.

Using List Brokers

Finding list brokers is relatively easy; telling a professional from the riffraff takes some experience. The best resource for finding a list broker is by reading the industry magazines, such as **DM News** (DM stands for Direct Marketing). According to Matt Gagnon (The Million Dollar Manual), here is a typical conversation when seeking a direct mail list:

"Hi, my name is John Smith, I run a small publishing business from my home, and I have a product that I would like to direct market. I am looking for a mailing list where the majority of people on it have purchased products similar to mine. I am on the market for about 75,000 to 90,000 names. I expect to pay $150 per thousand names. I would like those names printed on **Cheshire** peel-off labels. "

Depending on the broker, you will get responses similar to these:

1. "You want to pay that much? Do you have money to burn? I have names that are much cheaper, only $30.00 per thousand." *Click*, I have hung up already…

2. "We do not have that, but we can find it for you, for that we need to charge you $75 up front…" *Click*, I have just hung up on him, too….

3. "Yes, I think I have an idea what you are looking for. I can fax you a group of lists like that. They are going to be close, but if you wish to get an even closer match, I might be able to do a little more research. For that, I might need to charge you extra." **STAY ON THE LINE.**

The list owner pays mailing-list brokers. They typically get 10% to 15% of the price of the list, can, and do make other money from a list of additional services performed.

It is common to have two brokers involved with an acquisition of a list, the broker in charge of the list, and your broker, who found the list for you.

Some good list brokers will run the list against the online, postal database, and if the list comes back at over eighty percent valid, working addresses, then it can be considered a good one.

Same basics of using direct mailings:

• Make sure the purchasers on the list you obtain have paid similar prices for what you are offering.

• Purchase a list for 5,000 names. Brokers or list owners will not allow you to purchase any less. Do not mail out the entire 5,000 at once. Mail out

1,000 names and if the list is decent, you will make enough money from the first thousand to finance the mailing of the rest.

- Look for lists that are 50,000 to 75,000 strong.
- Make sure the list has purchasers and that they have actually **BOUGHT** goods or services you are selling.
- Buy only names of people that have purchased within the last six months, preferably, less than that. You do not want old lists! By the time any list matures to be one-year old, 15% of the addresses will be undeliverable. The post office usually forwards mail for only six months.

Seasonality of Marketing

I would not buy ads in August and in April. They are considered the worst months of the year for direct mail. Do not undertake any mailings in August, or in April, either.

Try to time your mailing so that it would not get to the prospect on a Monday. Monday is when all the other junk mail gets to them. Likely, they throw it all away, and your mail piece should not be among them.

Track your mail campaign

On the advertising piece you mail out, use a special code referencing the mailing list used. This way, you would know which mailing list(s) get good results. Ask the customers for the code. Always try to track your campaigns, so you know which lists work best, and so you can use them versus other, lesser-performing ones.

Internet Marketing

In 1992, there were fewer than 20,000 people on the Internet. Now this number is getting close to a billion.

Marketing on the Internet is not as cut and dried as off-line marketing. When the Internet was in its infancy, many people thought doing business, off-line would be completely altered by the advent of the Internet. People plowed millions of their hard-earned money into all sorts of dubious online business models. This was what we now refer to as the dot-com boom. Of course, after the boom, the bust followed.

There are a couple of points one must realize before embarking on any Internet-marketing plan:

- There are millions of websites now and for people to find yours, you must set yourself apart from the competition. You must offer first-class content and optimize for the search engines.

- Even if you follow the advice in the bullet above, getting noticed will take time. It will not happen overnight. Especially, if you do not have a PR Agency at your disposal, cannot afford prime-time TV ads, or full-page advertising in the **New York Times**.

- A modern website, in order to build a loyal and repeat readership, as well as a visitor base, must give something of value and it must give it away free. The days of one-page sales, letter-type[13],

---

[13] These are one-page web sites with only a sales copy to sell and nothing more. No free content which we view as essential

websites are over. There are literally hundreds of those, but they come and go. Again, free content rules. People like to see unique and valuable content when visiting a website. Hard selling and obvious websites have no chance.

Setting up a website

Despite the limitations and sobering facts of Internet, marketing, your business must have a website. There are exceptions to this rule. Some businesses do not require a website upon startup, but eventually, even the most mundane, brick-and-mortar style business should have a web presence.

Steps to take in setting up a website:

1.   Choose a domain name. Ideally, this domain name should be as short as possible, pertaining to your business, or trademark. The domain names each have a main body and a dot followed either by, **com, net**, or **org**. recently, the possible appendix after the dot has been expanded to **us, biz**, etc. Ignore all those. Choose a **.com** if possible. Try avoiding slashes in the name itself. The reason for this is obvious; Shakespeare asked, "What's in a name?" Well, in business on the Internet, the name is prestige, ease of remembering, and an identity. Long names with dashes have no chance of being memorable. Appendices, anything other than **.com** or **.org** are treated as cheesy, non-professional names. A **.org** is reserved for non-profit organizations and not to be used as individual or business sites. You can reserve a domain name at **go-**

daddy.com or some other registrars who **ICANN** accredits[14] to distribute domain names.

2.   Find a host for your domain name. A host is a company that has a bank of servers with fast Internet address and special software to enable your websites to function. Most host companies offer merchant account access to run credit card transactions, database servers to customize and tailor your websites to store data, and other scripts and software that enable your websites to gather leads and facilitate communications between you and customers.

3.   Find someone to put it all together for you. This person is ideally an experienced web master, specializing in customizing and building websites. He or she will have to build the webpages your websites will contain. Upload or **ftp** these files to the host companies' server, and perhaps even write and upload some content to your pages. This is also the time when the websites should be optimized to the search engines.

Once your website is ready, you want to show it to friends, and as many close acquaintances as possible. This is done in order to proofread and find typos, grammar mistakes, and other errors before you submit your website to the search engines. Ideally, the site should be error free.

---

[14] http://www.icann.org/en/registrars/accredited-list.html

Submitting to Search Engines

Before **Google** gained its dominance in the web search traffic, there were hundreds of search engines.

It was the task of the webmaster to submit, often manually, to all important search engines to be listed, or indexed/crawled by their "robots" or "web crawlers." If these words sound as alien to you as they do to me, then please read the following section on SEO (Search Engine Optimization)

Search Engine Optimization is the process of improving the volume and/or quality of traffic to a website by considering how search engines work and how people look for results.

Both parts of this must be considered when planning your SEO strategy; one without the other will garner great results for low-competitor search terms, or will return poor results for competitive search terms.

For example, if your website promoted the benefits of healthy eating, you may wish to be ranked for the term "healthy eating." This term is a very competitive one, with many thousands of companies all vying to have the best results for it.

However, if you were to optimize your site for the term "healthy eating will make me fitter," you would find that it was much easier to rank for this term--as there are fewer competitors wanting to be optimized for that term--but no person uses this as a search term.

In essence, you have created a strategy that will give you results that no other competitor is looking for. This is why you must have both facets of the process covered when considering your own SEO strategy.

How Do Search Engines Rank?

There are many different search engines, all using different techniques to determine how important your page is for a particular term, phrase, or subject.

The largest search engine is **Google**-- it uses a constantly evolving, dynamic algorithm to calculate the various positions for individual webpages. This algorithm is also secret.

Why Secret? Well, to put it plainly, if it were publicly available, it would be easier for search engine experts to tailor content, site structure, and more, in order to influence the ranking. Instead, **Google** tries to use the natural democratic nature of the Internet in order to drive its results.

PageRank™

Google uses the algorithm to rank pages on a scale between 0 and 10. Although the scale has almost infinite ranking positions, for ease of use, it only displays whole integers in the **PageRank** toolbar.

Each indexed webpage is assigned an individual ranking or level of importance by **Google,** based on a number of factors:

- **Back Links**

  Each time a site links to you, **Google** takes this as a "vote" for your site. The more links, the more votes, the better the rank.

It is not just the number of votes, though. If the **PageRank** of the site linking to yours is higher, then its vote is worth more. Therefore, a single link from a PR5 site is worth more than four links from PR1 sites.

- **Outbound Links**

There is a dark cloud to go with the silver lining. A page can only have one **PageRank** score. Moreover, every outbound link from that page (including internal links), takes a share of that ranking.

Therefore, if you have a link from a PR5 page, but that page has 99 other links, then you are only receiving 1/100th of the PR5. In this instance, a link from a PR1 page is actually better than the PR5 page link.

- **Outbound Link Quality**

You have no control over which sites link to you. For this reason, if you are linked to by an unsavory site (a link farm, banned content, pornography, etc.), your site is not penalized by **Google**.

However, you can control the quality of sites that you link to. For this reason, if you have an outbound link to an unsavory site, you will be penalized, and in extreme cases, removed from **Google**'s index completely.

- **Anchor Text**

Each link to your webpage requires an anchor. This can be an image or text that forms the hyperlink.

Google, and other search engines, look at the text used, or in the case of images, the **alt** text, to determine the nature of the link. This helps **Google** to determine what content your site is optimized for, and is one of the most under-used techniques in SEO.

Don't believe me? Try a search for "Click Here" in **Google**. What is the number one result? **Adobe Reader**.

Now open the page for **Adobe** (http://get.adobe.com/uk/reader/). Can you see the term "click here" anywhere on the page? No. It is not there. Yet it ranks #1 for the search term.

This is because many thousands of webpages have a link to the **Adobe** site with the anchor text "click here" in order to download the latest version of their **Reader** software. Remember this with your off-the-page SEO strategy (covered later in this article)

These techniques are predominantly off-the-page activities and will give the biggest SEO benefits. However, there are also many things that can be done on-the-page, which many people look to, to improve their page rankings on Google.

Off-The-Page and On-The-Page SEO

There are two methods of SEO that can be done--and they are not exclusive; you can, and should, do both.

On-the-page SEO covers all of the activities that you can do on your website. Off-the-page SEO covers all activities that are completed away from your website, on other webpages/sites.

We have already covered some of the off-the-page activities. The other main activities that you should do away from your site are:

- **Directory Submissions**

  Submit your website to all major directories. **DMOZ** is the main, free index, and should be considered for anyone that is serious about driving traffic.

  Of course, your site should also be submitted to and indexed by **Google, Yahoo!, Ask,** and **Bing** (formerly **MSN Search** and **Live Search**).

- **Article Submission**

  If your site has any amount of content (and it should), you should consider writing articles, press releases, and other documents for posting to article directories and news outlets.

  The articles should be keyword-rich (see On-The-Page) and include a link back to your site with suitable anchor text. These can be submitted to article sites such as **ezinearticles.com, article-hut.com** and even **digg.com**. You could even upload to **Facebook, Bebo** and other social networking sites, too.

On-the-page activities are much easier for you to control; not least of all, because they all take place within your own site.

As these are all within your control, they do not give as much benefit to your ranking as off-the-page SEO. However, many webmasters do not consider all on-the-page examples here, and they are missing some easy benefits.

- **Meta Tags**

Each webpage has several meta tags available. "Description," "Keywords," "Author," "last updated"--the list is immense.

Over the course of time, many of these tags have been abused by web developers and now are given varying levels of notice by the search engines. Some are ignored completely.

It is important to complete the following meta tags for your site:

meta name ="description" content = "your content here"

This tag provides the description that appears on your search engine result in **Google**. Although it has no (known) weight with ranking, it is presented to end users and should be interesting enough to make them click through to your site. It should be different for every page.

meta name ="title" content = "your content here"

Although not technically a meta tag, the title element is the single most important piece of information in the head section of your HTML.

The title helps **Google,** et al., to identify what your page is all about. It should be short and to the point, as the more words you have, the less their individual impact will be.

For example, if your title is three words long and contains the word "healthy," this will be regarded as the third most important search term in your page. If your page title is "healthy eating can make you thin," the word, "can" is just as important as the word "healthy," insofar as keyword density is concerned. **Google** seems to offer slightly more weight for words earlier in the sentence.

Each page title should be unique and relevant to your page. **Google** can penalize duplicate titles across pages.

meta name ="keywords" content = "your, content, here"

The keywords meta tag has been abused over the years and no longer has any importance to **Google**. However, some other search engines, such as **Yahoo!**, do still use the keywords tag and it should be added to all of your pages.

The other meta tags are primarily used to provide information to web developers, rather than to search engines. Some custom-made search engines will use tags such as "author" and "version." However, these are out of scope for this article.

- **HTML Structure**

Search engines love valid coding. The simpler your coding, the easier it is for the search engines to crawl your site content. And the easier it is to crawl, the easier it is to index your pages into the search engines.

In addition, web crawlers look at your page from the top down. So any additional coding in the header area (such as superfluous meta tags and javascript), actually reduces the crawler's ability to index your page content.

Adding your JavaScript calls to the bottom of your page (where possible), will not only speed up your page-load time for the user, it improves the crawler's efficiency, too.

- **CSS Structure**

Cascading Style Sheets allow your site content to be kept completely separate from your site styling.

As crawlers only look at your HTML--the content--having a valid CSS-driven site is beneficial to your SEO strategy.

- **Internal Anchor Text**

This is the most missed on-the-page strategy of all web developers.

Just as with external back links, each internal link has an image or text that forms your anchor. These can be optimized on your internal pages, too.

For example, if you have a "contact us" page, you can link to it with "click here." This will optimize the "contact us page" for the term "click here." This is clearly a poor idea.

Optimizing the anchor text to something such as "Contact Company name" is much better.

- **Content and Keywords**

The most important thing about your webpage is the content shown on it. **Google** knows it; your customers know it; you know it.

If your content contains the search phrases you wish to optimize for, it stands a far better chance of being ranked for those terms. Combined with the title element, this gives the biggest single benefit to your on-the-page program.

There are many other on-the-page activities that can be completed. **Alt** tags for images, clearing empty white space from your coding, and positioning of key phrases within your content, can all help to improve your ranking.

Summary

Search Engine Optimization was, at one time, a novelty that could be used to help to rank your site. Nowadays, with over 150 billion webpages online, SEO is no longer a choice.

If you want your site to be found by customers, you need to be able to position yourself within specific search terms, with quality content, and site structure.

As the search engines constantly hone their algorithms, this means that we, as designers, must also hone our own sites, our content, our back links, and our keywords. This will help to ensure that our sites continue to attract high-quality traffic from our search engine partners.

Back-end Marketing

Have you ever attended an inexpensive seminar or a workshop just to listen to a pitch on a more expensive course, a CD or DVD? The original seminar is typically, not useful or very informative and its sole purpose is to have a captive audience for selling a more expensive course or seminar.

This is what the industry calls, up selling. The idea behind it is that the audience is interested and motivated buyers otherwise; they would not have spent the time and money for the original event. I do not believe in tricks and unethical marketing, so my recommendation is to offer value, something tangible and worthwile; the buyers will most likely be also in the market for the up sell, the more expensive consulting offer that follows.

Lead Generation

When you are selling something, usually you work off a qualified list of leads. The leads are a list of people who have expressed interest in the subject matter you are selling. People sometimes purchase leads but the best way to generate leads is by doing it yourself. All you need is a one-page website with a nice URL, a good, professional sales copy to perk up the interest of the visitor and then a free offer of an ezine, a printed book or a pamphlet. This works differently in various businesses but all in all it works. Better to offer a tangible item such a book but you can offer a newsletter (of course, you must write one)

Chapter 5--Self-Promotion

Unless you hire a PR Agency, promoting your business will fall on you. Fortunately, this is not a full time job and certain businesses require less promotion than others do. Now you might ask this obvious question; what differentiates promotion from advertising. Promotion happens in a general context of the news media.

For example, a certain local but influential radio station expresses interest on doing a story on small businesses and you are selected to do the story. It takes 15 minutes on the telephone to do the interview.

After completing the interview, hundreds of thousands of listeners know your and your company's name; they also know what products or service you offer. They are free to look you up on the Internet and find out more. Usually, during the interview process the obvious advertising is intentionally left out. They would not publish 800 numbers and obvious references to the business that infomercials do.

The benefit of a low-keyed interview is that the audience is not as guarded during an informal interview as a radio commercial when he might even turn off the radio or tune into a different station.

How do you get an interview?

To be considered for an interview you must write a news release
When you launch your company
When you have a new product or a service.

You can either hire a professional to write your news release or you can give it a try yourself.

Disseminating your news release

The conventional and not so successful way of announcing your news release for the novice is putting it up on web sites such as PRWeb.com. I prefer to individually send it out to print and broadcast editors. You might want to purchase a database such as *Publicity Blitz Media Directory-on-Disk* (works both on a PC or Apple); it lists 20,000 print and broadcast editors.

Hints for doing a successful radio interview

Use "ear" words instead of "eye" words, promotions for radio is unique because your content is not about how things sound in your mind when reading. It is all about how it sounds when read aloud. When you are interviewed, your phrasing should be pleasing to the ear. Use short sentences. Spoken word in a radio interview is linear. Unlike a newspaper article or a web page, where the eye can take in an entire page quickly, the ear only processes the message of a radio interview as it is spoken.

Tips on Writing a News Release

Start your news release with an effective headline. You should write a headline that would capture the attention of the editor as the readers should the editor decide to print it in a newspaper.

Keep the news release to one page. Write double spaced. If you go over one page, edit out what does not fit in.

Focus on the general benefit of your business while enhancing what differentiates you from the competition.

Use ample quotes from customers, clients.

How to Write a Good Press Release

A press release, also known as a *news release*, is simply a written announcement to the media. They can communicate a range of news items: scheduled events, personnel promotions, awards, new products and services, sales accomplishments, etc.

A well-crafted press release can also help in generating a feature story. Reporters are more likely to consider a story idea if they first receive a release. A good press release is a fundamental tool of promotional work, one that anyone who is willing to use the proper format can use.

A news release comprises of

- Headline
- Body
- Contact

News release headlines should have an attention grabber characteristic to captivate the readers, i.e., journalists, just as a newspaper headline purports to attract readers. It may describe the latest achievement of an organization, a recent newsworthy event, a new product or service.

Headlines should be in bold and are typically larger than the press release text. Conventional press release headlines are present tense and exclude "a" and "the" as well as forms of the verb "to be" in certain contexts.

The first word in the press release headline should be capitalized, as should all proper nouns. Most headline words appear in lower-case letters, although adding a stylized "small caps" style can create a more graphically news-attractive look and feel. Do not capitalize every word.

The press release should be in block style, so no paragraph indentation is necessary. Keep the tone of your release all business. Do not go into too much personal or non-business related detail or your press release will likely end up in the editor's garbage bin.

The simplest method to arrive at the press release headline is to extract the most important keywords from your press release. Now from these keywords, try to frame a logical and attention-getting statement. Using keywords will give you better visibility in search engines, and it will be simpler for journalists and readers to get the idea of the press release content.

Write the press release body copy. You should write the press release, as you want it to appear in a news story.

Start with the date and city in which the press release is originated. The city may be omitted if it were confusing, for example if the release is written in San Francisco about events in the company's new Florida division.

The lead, or first sentence, should grab the reader and say concisely what is happening. The next 1-2 sentences then expand upon the lead.

The press release *body copy* should be compact. Avoid using very long sentences and paragraphs. Avoid repetition and over use of fancy language and jargon.

A first paragraph (two to three sentences) must actually sum up the press release and the further content must elaborate it. In a fast-paced world, neither journalists nor other readers would read the entire press release if the start of the article did not generate interest.

Deal with facts - events, products, services, people, targets, goals, plans, projects. Try to provide maximum use of concrete facts. A simple method for writing an effective press release is to keep in mind of the following:

Communicate the five Ws and the H. Who, what, when, where, why, and how. Then consider the points below if pertinent.

- What is the actual news?
- Why this is news?
- The people, products, items, dates and other things related with the news.
- The purpose behind the news.
- Your company - the source of this news.

Now from the points gathered, try to construct paragraphs and assemble them sequentially: The headline > the summary or introduction of the news > event or achievements > product > people > again the concluding summary > the company.

The length of a press release should be no more than three pages. If you are sending a hard copy, text should be double-spaced.

The more newsworthy you make the press release copy, the better the chances of it being selected by a journalist or reporting. Find out what "newsworthy" means to a given market and use it to hook the editor or reporter.

Include information about the company. When a journalist picks up your press release for a story, he/she would logically have to mention the company in the news article. Journalists can then get the company information from this section.

The title for this section should be - About XYZ_COMPANY

After the title, use a paragraph or two to describe your company with 5/6 lines each. The text must describe your company, its core business and the business policy. Many businesses already have professionally written brochures, presentations, and business plans – place that introductory text can here.

At the end of this section, point to your website. The link should be the exact and complete URL without any embedding so that, even if this page is printed, the link will be show as it is.

For example; http://www.your_company_website.com

Companies that maintain a separate media page on their websites must point to that URL here. A media page typically has contact information and press kits.

Contact information.

If your press release were newsworthy, journalists would surely like more information or would like to interview key people associated with it.

If you are comfortable with the idea of letting your key people contacted by media, you can provide their contact details on the press release page itself. For example, in case of some innovation, you can provide the contact information of your engineering or research team for the media.

Otherwise, you must provide the details of your media/PR department in the "Contact" section. If you do not have dedicated team for this function, you must appoint somebody who will act as a link between the media and your people.

1. The contact details must be limited and specific only to the current press release. The contact details must include:
   The Company's Official Name
2. Media Department's official Name and Contact

Person
3. Office Address
4. Telephone and fax Numbers with proper country/city codes and extension numbers
5. Mobile Phone Number (optional)
6. Timings of availability
7. E-mail Addresses
8. Web site Address

Denote the end of the press release with three # symbols, centered directly underneath the last line of the release. This is a journalistic standard.

Usefull Tips

If the press release is for immediate release, you could write "IMMEDIATE RELEASE" in all caps on the left margin, directly above the headline. If you wish to delay the press release until a further date, put "EMBARGOED UNTIL..." with the date you want the story released. Omission of release date implies immediate release.

Try to research actual press releases on the web to get the feel of the tone, the language, the structure and the format of a good press release.

The timing of the press release is very important. It must be relevant and recent news, not too old and not too distant. A follow-up call can help develop a press release into a full story.

Include a "call to action" in your release. This is information on what you want the public to do with the information that you are releasing. For example, do you want them to buy a product? If so, include information on where the product is available. Do you want them to visit your Web site to enter a contest or learn more about your organization? If so, include the Web address or a phone number.

Do not waste time writing the headline until you finish writing the whole release. When you have finished a draft of the release, and then think about the headline.

Send your release by e-mail, and use formatting sparingly. Giant type and multiple colors do not enhance your news, they distract from it. Put the news release in the body of the e-mail, not as an attachment. Word documents are acceptable at most outlets, but if you are using the newest version (.docx), save down a version (.doc). Newspapers, especially, are on tight budgets now, and many have not upgraded. Use PDF files only if you are sending a full media kit with lots of graphics.

Appendix A--Business Plan Writing

This is a brief outline of a business plan that, should you require financing or angel investors, you as the small businessperson might want to write.

If you were a manager who has to administer to several junior staff members, you would expect each member of your staff to provide you with a written report on the progress. This report must show any profits, costs, productivity, as well as suggestions for the next few months. Always keep an informal and easy-to-read style of writing. But be professional, keeping your readers in mind and clarifying what needs to be done, rather than just assuming things.

The plan should provide a way to organize effort and resources to achieve a desired outcome. In a business context, a plan's numerical data, including costs and revenues, are normally scheduled over at least one trading year, broken down weekly, monthly, quarterly, and cumulatively.

Always use a clear, standard format and comprising an explanation, justification, and relevant numerical and financial statistical data to allow the readers to find the information they need quickly and easily. The report must provide the company with a clear map, with milestones against which the progress can be monitored, or evaluated. It must have in-depth analysis, research and planning, and the format should allow your information to be delivered through proper, logical steps, so that the readers will be able to read and follow with ease. Always be sure to have a clear understanding of the reason for writing the report, and make sure it is just as clear to the people reading it.

Executive Summary

Always mention the most important thing first and be clear about what you are trying to say. The main aim of this summary is to solve any problems prior to making any costly purchases, installations, and/or any other alterations. This will be the first step to work towards developing a profitable business.

Introduction

This would mention the report name, your business details, owner's name, management staff, and date, etc. You need to tell people about the continued success and future benefits, as well as opportunities for both the consumer and commercial market.

When offering your customers a service, always explain how it works and what specific need it fulfills in the marketplace, as well as any contribution towards helping the environment. If you are selling a product, then explain its function, characteristics, and usefulness. You can also explain how it is produced from recycled material, and the type of labor needed.

Internal Factors

You can mention how various measures can be taken to insure business sustainability and growth. You can explain how to resolve many problems by interacting with customers. This will also include the review of the company's promotional programs and the assessment of the image and reputation of the company.

Target Markets, Growth Strategies and SWOT Analysis

As a result of many technological advances, businesses these days are experiencing many changes. The report should mention, as to how this will affect the market, and where the focus of emergent vendor activity will be strongest.

You can also mention various weaknesses, such as limited marketing budget, etc.

External Factors

Give details about various challenges, main competitors, and also how to enhance business by targeting a specific area. This may also include various environmental factors, as well, and how possible climate changes might affect the productivity.

Strategy and Implementation Summary

Explain the growth and progress of the business briefly under this heading.

Marketing Strategy

You can give details of any special marketing program, such as offers of discounts and deals.

Promotion Strategy

This would explain various plans to promote the products or services to customers.

Distribution Strategy

This must include the main marketing campaign and the estimated costs for this campaign.

Sales Strategy

Give the details of the staff and any special sales strategies that have been put in place.

Personnel Plan

The responsibilities of the owner and all the employees, according to their performance and experience, can be mentioned here in detail. You can explain, briefly, the problem you are trying to solve, describe the most important information or results, and give any action steps that you suggest.

Break-Even Analysis

This can be calculated on the average of the first-year figures for total sales by units, and by running expenses, including rent, utilities, payroll, etc.

Projected Profit and Loss

Estimated increase in sales for coming months and years can be calculated.

Projected Cash Flow

This is an estimate as to whether the business is generating enough cash to support all the expenses and meeting the needs of the business and the staff.

Expense Budget Analysis

You can explain how an increase in sales can help reduce the expenses.

Milestones

Aims and ambitions may differ, as some companies would focus on quality[15] and meeting particular targets[16] and standards, whereas others would want to survive and make profits.

---

[15] http://www.thetimes100.co.uk/glossary--quality-1172.php
[16] http://www.thetimes100.co.uk/glossary--targets-1429.php

Appendix B--Working, Home, and Education

Working at home and homeschooling your children may seem like a daunting task, but this article is to help you see that it is really quite ordinary and easy to do.

More and more people are home schooling their kids than ever. I would like to take a moment of your time to show you the pros and cons of homeschooling and how one might successfully integrate it with your work life.

Having a busy work life, you may want to take advantage of this unique opportunity. Home schooling has changed drastically through the years from the perspective that children are taught directly from their parents. To the idea, that given all the tools necessary they can learn for themselves with a guiding hand along the way.

With correspondence schools, you are giving your kids a formal education split up into courses, this is called a curriculum. The materials are provided by the correspondence schools and the children work with the materials. In a way, they are learning to teach themselves with the tools provided, which is what can make a home school experience so valuable and a viable solution for working at home.

Homeschooling Internationally

Did you know, over three million children are taught right in their own homes. In North America, the option of homeschooling is much more lenient than many other countries like Brazil, China, and Germany, to name a few. Countries with a growing population base of homeschooling include Australia, Canada, New Zealand, United Kingdom and United states. Some countries have chosen to ban it entirely.

Many people worldwide are realizing that this life style change could be the wave of the future, allowing them to adapt to a world where economic stresses are more prominent than ever.

How Will I Save?

So you got to be asking yourself what this can do for you financially. Many people are starting to work at home, and choosing to save the money they would normally spend on daycare. They can use the same money that is being given for inadequate schooling for the kids, and use the money for specialized home care. Your kids then receive the specialized care they should be getting in the first place; as well as the supervision and patience that your child deserves. Not to mention every year parents spend hundreds of dollars on back to school supplies. Granted you will still need to buy many of the same supplies, but you may save on the accessories and monthly expenses.

Planning for Consistency

It is important above all to be consistent in the plan. Setting up a schedule for how you would like the plan to work and then following through. Your children need to be able to count on you, but you must also be able to count on your children. It is a good idea to set them down and be firm on the rules and what should be done on their own. One of the biggest lessons learned by most homeschoolers is independence and how to respond maturely in their home environment.

Being able to make adjustments to your schedule is the benefit to this program, but adjust with moderation. Education and interruption rarely go hand in hand. Your children deserve consistency in their education; they thrive on learning and can do it easily given the right conditions. Remember, this is your choice... discover what works best for you as well as gets the best quality of education.

Options Available to You

The teaching tools often differ from the different correspondence schools. There are different teaching styles that can be offered if one simply is not working. It is not unusual for you to mail test and quizzes across the country. The work is completed and sent back to the school for official review, graded by real teachers and sent back. This is typical, but the methods for teaching can differ.

In one scenario, they use video correspondence, where they had real classrooms on film with real teachers and classmates. The experience is very similar to a typical classroom. With this teaching style, there is often a sense of connection with the remote classroom. Being on video has the added attraction that they can edit out the nonsense that you may try to avoid in regular schools, the video teachers are very personal so you may gain experience from their stories.

Another Example...

Other correspondence schools may not have the advantage of audio/video; however, they can be primarily textbooks for reading and filling out the related tests or quizzes. This may be okay in some classes, while other classes that are more demanding like Algebra could be a nightmare in this format.

This method of learning can be increasingly difficult to maintain a child's interest and may require more third party involvement from the parent. Therefore, this is something to consider when choosing a correspondence school. One advantage of this type of education though is cost, so this option may depend on your budget. If you can afford it, it is recommended going with a more intuitive setup like video.

Online classes are also there for consideration with a variety ranging from chat to video conference. If using the method it is advised, you set up software to prohibit the use of browsing or running applications. As we all know, the internet and computer alone are a playground for distractions.

What are the Challenges?

Obstacles

The work errands are inevitable, so long as you get the ball rolling again when you return, this generally still works out. We must also consider the development of the kid, is he/she well behaved or do they act out a lot? Home schooling may reduce these behavioral problems as your kids are taken away from other children with neglected problems. Home school can reduce the stress of your child, and in turn the stress upon you and your work. This may also depend on the attention of your child.

Social Factors

Though there really is no substitute for interaction, with a little creativity and planning you can easily compensate for the social shortcomings, if any. Homeschooling can take up less time for your child, depending on how motivated he or she is. Most home schooled kids will finish their daily courses within a very reasonable period.

This gives time to work on other activities they enjoy, or to finish more schoolwork in advance. The added bonus of having free time could work in your favor, giving them time to be engaged in sports or hobbies that will keep them occupied while you work.

Work & Home Boundaries between Work and Home

Also keep in mind, the proximity of where you decide to work at home and the location of where your child has set up can make a difference. If you are too close, your child may not earn a sense of independence. They have to know that they are accomplishing this on their own. Too far away and unsupervised you are giving them too much free reign to do things besides schoolwork. It is healthy to set up boundaries for your child's schoolwork. Setting aside a room and a space for their schoolwork gives it a more official tone that you may want to keep. Creating the atmosphere for school can go a long way.

What are the Advantages?

Quality Care

With all of the horror stories of incidents that go on at public institutions, it is really no wonder many people are switching to home school. Our children really are the products of our environment. We like to coach our kids on how to dress, what to eat, what time to sleep. Yet when we send them to a public daycare provider, it is important to know what kind of environment we are subjecting to our little ones. I think most of us prefer to have as little question as possible on how our kids are being raised. That is where home schooling can come in, to help alleviate unwanted outside influences. The question is... do you want your children to aspire to learn to be more like you? Or the spiky haired foul mouth kid he sits next to?

Measuring Performance

They will still be required to take SAT and ACT tests to advance, you may have to locate one of these testing facilities, but the frequencies of these tests are not enough to be an issue.

This can be done in facilities designed to take on homeschoolers in large groups, but there are also more privatized setups that take fewer kids to complete the tests. These tests grade the achievement of your child to compare with other children. This will allow you to review what classes that need to be given more attention.

About Credits

Like college, you also get to choose which courses you would like your child to take this gives you more flexibility over what you want your children to learn and which order you would like them to learn it. The individual courses then add up to equal credits, each course is worth a different amount of credits. Often they are worth one credit. Another aspect you may be interested in is that, depending on which correspondence school you attend. Your child may be able to graduate earlier. Some correspondence schools require fewer credits than others to graduate. Generally, this is equivalent to getting your GED but through a school.

Scheduling for Success

It is also a good idea to set timetables for your kids, for example. Setting a rule, that school starts at 8am and no less than X amount of hours. It is important that some amount of order is kept. This way you can attend to your own work duties without being interrupted.

If you have multiple children, it is desirable to seek the outside help of a babysitter. Even the teachers at regular schooling facilities have assistants, why not you too? The more children you have the more unpredictable your education demands become. You may decide to reserve the babysitter for important dates on your work schedule if budget becomes a factor. However keeping in mind the money you will be saving in the long run it may help pay the wages of hiring the outside help.

Your work may be interrupted but with the proper atmosphere and planning, your day should amount with minimal amounts of stress, allowing you get the work you need done while your children minding their studies.

We all lead different lives and what activities we have set up throughout your day-to-day may interfere with your ability to be there for your children. If you are in the position where you are at home for the majority of the day, the homeschooling option can be most beneficial.

Conclusion

By the end of this Chapter, I hope I have put your mind at ease; it is really not that difficult as it may look or sound. Remember to relax and enjoy the reason for your homeschooling is to enjoy the time with your kids and learn together. The average teacher may spend 7 hours a day teaching a dozen children. This is equal to tutoring one child one or two hours a day. Learning is always a lot easier when in a relaxed environment with one on one attention.

It is helpful to talk to people who already have homeschooled their children. They will have plenty of advice to get you started. If you do not know, anyone find an online support group. Next, find out the different laws in your state or country.

Above all, you must have fun. There may be times you are feeling frustrated, but do not worry, homeschooling should be about learning at home, not taking your school into your home.

Relax, be productive, and enjoy your children.

Index

www.ingramcontent.com/pod-product-compliance
Lightning Source LLC
Chambersburg PA
CBHW050125280326
41933CB00010B/1251